The Excuse Encyclopedia

Copyright © 2021 by James Warwood

Published by Amazon.

All rights reserved.

No part of this book may be used, stored or reproduced in any manner whatsoever without written permission from the author or publisher.

Book cover design by: Camille Rejenne Pavon
Book interior design by: Mala Letra / Lic. Sara F. Salomon

ISBN 978-1-915646-31-6
ebook ISBN B08NH2IZK2

The Excuse Encyclopedia

BOOK 1 49 EXCUSES FOR NOT TIDYING YOUR BEDROOM — 7

BOOK 2 49 WAYS TO STEAL THE COOKIE JAR — 75

BOOK 3 49 EXCUSES FOR NOT DOING YOUR HOMEWORK — 139

BOOK 4 49 QUESTIONS TO ANNOY YOUR PARENTS — 207

BOOK 5 49 EXCUSES FOR SKIPPING GYM CLASS — 267

BOOK 6 49 EXCUSES FOR STAYING UP PAST YOUR BEDTIME — 331

BOOK 7 49 EXCUSES FOR BEING REALLY LATE — 395

BOOK 8 49 EXCUSES FOR NOT EATING YOUR VEGETABLES — 461

BOOK 9 49 EXCUSES FOR NOT DOING YOUR CHORES — 525

BOOK 10 49 EXCUSES FOR GETTING THE MOST OUT OF CHRISTMAS — 603

BOOK 11 49 EXCUSES FOR EXTENDING YOUR SUMMER HOLIDAY — 679

BOOK 12 49 EXCUSES FOR BAGGING MORE CANDY AT HALLOWEEN — 751

ABOUT THE AUTHOR — 815

BOOK ONE

Excuses for Not Tidying Your Bedroom

Book I: Bedroom Excuses

1 THE (MAKE-BELIEVE) FRIENDS EXCUSE

My imaginary friends are tidying my room as we speak . . .

. . . Laura is dusting. Boris is tidying up. Jenny is searching for my other green sock. Ronald is hoovering, but you can't hear him because he's using an invisible hoover.

2. THE INFECTIOUS EXCUSE

I've got Multi-Coloured Chicken Pox! . . .

. . . my body is covered in red, green, blue and orange spots. It says on this felt tip pen that multi-coloured chicken pox is highly contagious and that the infected child should rest until the spots fade away. As these are new felt tip pens I suspect I'm going to be ill for a long time.

Book 1: Bedroom Excuses

3. THE ACTIVIST EXCUSE

I'm on a Tidiness Strike. So far I haven't lifted a finger for 8 days, 15 hours and 47 seconds...

... well someone's got to speak up for Caterpillar Rights.

4. THE MASTERPIECE EXCUSE

I've become a Contemporary Modern Artist. This is my latest work, I call it 'The Untidy Room of a Young Genius'...

...I reckon some French millionaire should arrive any minute now to buy my masterpiece. So don't touch ANYTHING!!!

Book I: Bedroom Excuses

5. THE UPSET STOMACH EXCUSE

I can't tidy my room because I've got butterflies in my stomach . . .

. . . I should never have eaten that Caterpillar Sandwich for lunch!

The Excuse Encyclopedia

6. THE OVER-PHOBIC EXCUSE

Help!

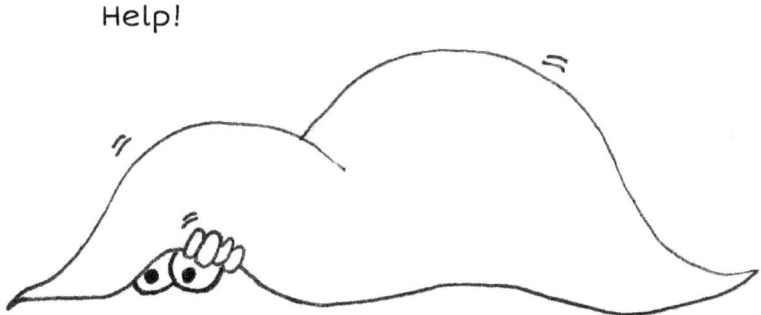

... There's a spider[1] under my bed. It's teasing me because I'm too scared to play Scrabble[2], Go Fish[3], Snap[4], , Twister[5], Hungry Hippos[6], Battleships[7], and Guess Who[8][9][10] and then it called me Floccinaucinihilipilification.[11]

---

[1] Arachnophobia - fear of spiders.
[2] Verbophobia - fear of words.
[3] Ichthyophobia - fear of fish.
[4] Ligyrophobia - fear of loud noises.
[5] Chromatophobia - fear of colours.
[6] Phagophobia - fear of swallowing or of eating or of being eaten.
[7] Arithmophobia - fear of numbers.
[8] Peladophobia - fear of bald people.
[9] Pogonophobia - fear of beards.
[10] Xenophobia - fear of strangers or foreigners.
[11] Hippopotomonstrosesquipedaliophobia - fear of long words (and hippos).

Book 1: Bedroom Excuses

7. THE SPIRITUAL EXCUSE

Thanks to meditation I've discovered my deeply spiritual inner self that doesn't require a tidy bedroom to experience lasting happiness and inner peace...

... you look stressed, maybe you should try it too.

8. THE REVISION EXCUSE

Sorry but I'm revising for my spelling test tomorrow . . .

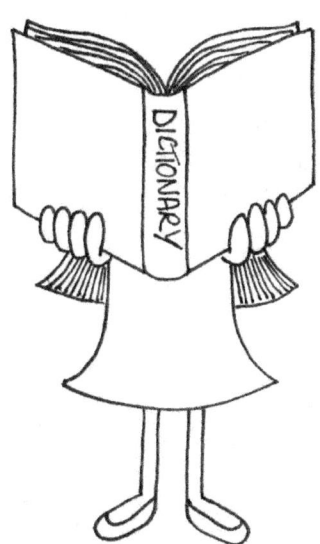

. . . I know it's only a 10 word test, but Miss Print said there will be a surprise bonus word. So I decided to be thorough and learn all 60,000 words in the English Dictionary.

Book I: Bedroom Excuses

9. THE NEW BUSINESS EXCUSE

Welcome to my new business venture. I call it...

... I'd be happy to mess up your bedroom as well, for a small fee.

The Excuse Encyclopedia

10. THE IMPORTANT RESEARCH EXCUSE

Aaaaaaaargh! You made me lose count! . . .

. . . I am doing some very important research for AbsolutelyPointlessFacts.com, counting how many toes a centipede has. Now I'll have to start all over again. 1, 2, 3 . . .

11. PROFESSIONAL DEVELOPMENT EXCUSE

A career advisor visited our school yesterday and told us to start practicing what we want to be when we grow up . . .

. . . so I'm practicing being unemployed. I'm already very good at sleeping in past lunch time and I've mastered not tidying my bedroom, so next on my professional development list is to watch TV all day and shout at the neighbour's cat.

The Excuse Encyclopedia

12. THE PARENT-CHILD-SWITCH-A-ROO EXCUSE

Have the court papers not arrived yet? I've adopted you . . .

. . . so go tidy your room! And lights out at 8:30pm

Book I: Bedroom Excuses

13. THE ZOMBIE INVASION EXCUSE

Don't panic. Zombies have taken over the entire town, surrounded the house and are about to . . . SMASH!!!

. . . . they've broken in! Quickly lock yourselves in the basement. I'll fight them off with the inflatable baseball bat I won at the Carnival.

14. THE PLAGUE OF QUESTION MARKS EXCUSE

These question marks are refusing to leave until I've solved the greatest mystery in the known universe: 'The Meaning of Life'...

... this could take 8-10 years so tidying my bedroom will have to wait.

Book I: Bedroom Excuses

15. THE FAR-TOO-BUSY EXCUSE

I can't tidy my room, my schedule is jam-packed . . .

. . . I've got a board meeting at 9am, a multi-million project to plan and a mountain of emails to reply to. You'll have to speak with my secretary, Mrs Potato Head, she'll pencil it into my diary early next week.

16. THE SCIENTIFIC EXCUSE

Did you know that a recent scientific study has shown that 92% of children who never tidied their rooms achieved better grades in schools, grew up to become the worlds most successful and happy people . . .

. . . If you don't believe me then email the scientist. His name is Dr Goggle.

17. THE NATURE LOVER EXCUSE

 I just received a letter from the Government declaring that my bedroom has become a Protected Nature Reserve for several species of endangered bacteria . . .

 . . . so if I tidy my room I'll be breaking the law. You've always taught me to live within the law of this great nation, so for the protection of these microscopic germs I promise to never tidy my bedroom ever again.

18. THE CLEVER NEW WORD EXCUSE

I learnt a new word at school this week, 'delegation'...

...now I shall explain what it means with a demonstration. Dad, fold up my clothes. Mum, pick up all my Lego. When you're finished come back to me for another demonstration.

Book 1: Bedroom Excuses

19. THE RECORD BREAKER EXCUSE

Harry is currently attempting the World Record for the longest whistle...

...DO NOT DISTURB!!!

20. THE TACTICAL TANTRUM EXCUSE

You should be warned . . .

. . . I've finished my tactical tantrum course, graduated top of my class and received my degree in 'Getting What I Want All The Time.'

21. THE RICH KID EXCUSE

I've given up being a little kid to become a handsome billionaire . . .

. . . so one of my many servants will tidy my room shortly and give you a complimentary back massage for your inconvenience.

22. THE MOST POWERFUL WIZARD EXCUSE

Be quiet Muggles! I've found the Elder Wand and fixed it with Sellotape from the kitchen drawer. I am now the most powerful wizard in the world . . .

. . . what's the spell to make it rain Chocolate Frogs?

Book I: Bedroom Excuses

23. TREAT YOUR PARENTS TO A HOLIDAY EXCUSE

I know you're both very stressed from raising a lazy son, so I've booked us an all-expenses paid holiday to Disney Land . . .

. . . don't worry about the money. I used your credit card.

24. THE EVIL TWIN EXCUSE

I'm your daughter's evil twin sister . . .

. . . I've come to sabotage her tidy reputation. Now if you would excuse me all this sabotaging has made me peckish. Which way to the fridge?

Book 1: Bedroom Excuses

25. THE ALLERGIES EXCUSE

I've had a severe allergic reaction to clean air, so please don't tidy my room. It's the only thing keeping me alive! . . .

. . . I would lift my bedding to show you the grotesque rash across my body but I've also recently discovered that I'm allergic to lifting as well.

26. THE FAKE DOCUMENTARY EXCUSE

I hope you don't mind but I've signed our family up to be on a documentary. It's called 'The Strictest Parents on the Planet and their Long-Suffering Children' . . .

. . . this is Steve the camera man, he'll be recording everything you do and say 24 hours a day 7 days a week. Well don't be rude, say hello.

Book I: Bedroom Excuses

27. THE MILITARY COUP EXCUSE

While you have been busying yourselves with everyday life I have been raising an army, a Bathroom Army. I DECLARE WAR! . . .

. . . Octopus of Terror, capture my spotty sister's room. Rubber Ducky Regiment, lay siege to the kitchen then sweep through the downstairs kingdoms. I shall lead the Toothbrush Squadron and the Bleach Cannons to the Throne Room and take this Household as mine.

28. THE GHOSTLY EXCUSE

Whoooooooooooooooo. Whooooooooooooooo. Whoooooooooooooooooooooo. I am the Ghost of Christmas Present . . .

. . . What? It isn't Christmas yet? Oh, my mistake, I'll be going then. Be sure to save me some turkey and a Christmas Cracker on my return.

Book 1: Bedroom Excuses

29. THE AMATEUR ASTRONAUT EXCUSE

How can I tidy my room when my head is full of curiosity? I'm tired of the theories. I'm sick of the rumours. I need to know . . .

. . . is the moon made of cheese? It will be the most important scientific breakthrough since the 'Heated Toilet Seat'. If I'm not back in time for dinner, leave me some in the microwave please.

The Excuse Encyclopedia

30. THE TEAMWORK EXCUSE

My teacher told me to practice working as a team . . .

. . . Mum, pick up all my dirty washing and then take my dirty cups to the kitchen. Dad, tidy my bed and then hoover the carpet. I'll water my imaginary cactus with my imaginary watering can until you're done.

Book I: Bedroom Excuses

31. THE EVE OF HIBERNATION EXCUSE

It'll have to wait till next year because winter is fast approaching. It's time to hang up my work boots and hibernate . . .

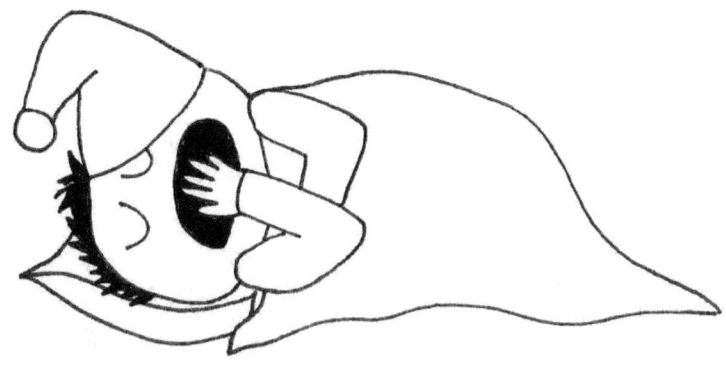

. . . didn't you know I'm part-human, part-squirrel. Wake me up when American Idol is back on.

32. THE RELIGIOUS CONVERT EXCUSE

I've been converted to Crispyanity...

...my religion commands me to follow the 'Crisps, Crisps & More Crisps' diet, to never tidy my room, to stand up and salute every crisp TV advert and collect empty crisps packets as offerings to the Potato God.

Book I: Bedroom Excuses

33. THE ADVICE FROM MY THERAPIST EXCUSE

The therapist you hired to cure my Compulsive Lying Disorder thinks I need a holiday in Hawaii to learn how to surf and become a limbo champion . . .

. . . she also thinks you should pay.

The Excuse Encyclopedia

34. THE CHANGE OF CAREER EXCUSE

You always call me a cheeky monkey so I finally took your advice and became the Monk who looks after all the keys to the Monastery...

... you should see my bedroom in the monastery, it's spotless! Plus if I'm invited to a Star Wars themed Birthday Party I only need the ears and I could go as Yoda.

Book I: Bedroom Excuses

35. THE UNDER-PAR PARENTING EXCUSE

Rule 179 in 'The Good Parenting Guide' clearly states "when telling your daughter to go and clean her bedroom you must place your left hand on your hip, point to the bedroom with our righthand, and shoot lasers through your eyes burning two holes in her soul" . . .

. . . now go upstairs, learn this guide off-by-heart and practice, practice, practice. I'll be in my messy bedroom when you're ready.

The Excuse Encyclopedia

36. THE RIDDLER EXCUSE

Ok I'll tidy my room, but first a riddle . . .

. . . the beginning of eternity, the end of time and space, the beginning of every end, and the end of every place. What am I? . . .

. . . THE LETTER 'E'.

Book 1: Bedroom Excuses

37. THE PLAYGROUND EXCUSE

I would tidy my room but I'm stuck in the mud . . .

. . . someone tagged me just as I was leaving school and I had to waddle home like this!

38. THE TEACHERS ADVICE EXCUSE

My teacher told me I should take a long hard look at myself...

...I decided to start from my shoes and work up. So far I'm up to my belt buckle which means this homework should take another hour or two.

Book I: Bedroom Excuses

39. THE PRANKSTER EXCUSE

Please, sit down. I have an important announcement to make...

...FAAAAAAAART! I put Woppie Cushions on your chairs. Hehehe.

40. THE ALMOST WORLD CHAMPION EXCUSE

But I can't tidy my room! Look at this...

... I'm 4th in the Angry Birds World Rankings, just 7 points away from being the best bird flinger in the entire world! So I think you'll agree this is far more important than something as trivial as 'tidying'.

41. THE SUPERHERO EXPERIMENT EXCUSE

I've been spending all my time genetically mutating this centipede, then I've been leaving it's cage open and pretending to take a photo of this cardboard cut-out of Mary Jane...

...just imagine having 100 arms and legs! I could tidy my room, play computer games and update my Facebook status all at the same time.

42. THE SECRET AGENT EXCUSE

Just got a call from MI6. James Bond is on his holidays so they've asked me to be his replacement...

... by the way this phone is due to self-destruct in 5 seconds. Would you put it in the outside bin for me as I've got to go and save the world!

Book 1: Bedroom Excuses

43. THE ROCK STAR EXCUSE

Haven't you heard the big news? My band - 'The Teddy Bears' - just signed a record deal after head lining at the Church Annual Picnic . . .

. . . so I figured a bunch of screaming fans will storm into my room any second now, looking for anything they can take home to make a shrine in their bedrooms.

44. THE PARENT-CHILD PEACE AGREEMENT EXCUSE

I think you'll find I cleaned my bedroom in March this year . . .

. . . It's only October now and as you well know the Child-Parent Peace Agreement of 2011 clearly states 'children only have to clean their bedrooms once a year'. Don't make me call the UN.

Book I: Bedroom Excuses

45. THE PPP EXCUSE

The PPP (Pushy Parents Police) just called and threatened to throw you guys in prison for 'Repeated-Harassment, Kissing in Public & Wearing Odd Socks Outside the House' . . .

. . . but don't panic, I told them you were taking me to the beach for ice cream today so you're off the hook. But be warned, next time I won't be so lenient!

46. THE LOST BOY EXCUSE

I've been in Neverland for the past 6 months and the first thing you say is 'tidy your room' . . .

. . . haven't you missed me? I used up all my fairy dust from Tinkerbell to come home! Where's my hug!?

Book 1: Bedroom Excuses

47. THE ROCK & ROLL EXCUSE

Have you heard of the drummer from 'The Who' (a band from the 1960's your parents would have loved) He's called Keith Moon? . . .

. . . apparently he once drove a Bentley into a swimming pool and he trashed every hotel room he ever stayed in! So I imagine that compared to Mr Moon's bedroom, mine is extremely tidy. While we're on the subject could we convert the garden into a swimming pool and convert my sister's room into my new drumming room?

The Excuse Encyclopedia

48. THE FORCE-FIELD EXCUSE

Really... well I've forged an invisible anti-adult force-field around my entire bedroom...

... if you try to step in here you'll immediately turn into a pile of dust! Go ahead, step into my room and see if I'm bluffing.

Book I: Bedroom Excuses

49. THE RITE OF PASSAGE EXCUSE

Look, I get it. Tidying my bedroom is a rite of passage that all children must go through . . .

. . . Your parents told you to tidy your bedroom and their parents told them to tidy their bedroom and on and on it continues. This will teach me the importance of responsibility and cleanliness and integrity that I will carry with me into adulthood (and then one day I will have sweet revenge on my children by telling them to tidy their bedrooms). So, I'll do it, as long as you wipe that smile off your face and give me a hand.

BONUS: NEW YOGA POSITION EXCUSE

Can't you tell? . . .

Yoga Position: 'the Lazy Slop'

. . . I'm in the middle of a yoga session. In fact, I'm so good I've invented my own yoga position (and mastered it). Tidying my room will ruin the inner tranquillity I've been working so hard to strengthen, plus the Teenage Mutant Ninja Turtles is on.

BONUS: SPOT EXCUSE

I can't tidy my bedroom . . .

. . . Why? Because if I move from this spot the world will end! So, I'm going to need you to get me a can of coke with a big straw and angle the TV towards me. The entire population of the world thanks you.

BONUS: STARFISH EXCUSE

I've been trying to tidying my bedroom all day . . .

. . . But I've lost my sight, smell, taste and hearing due to a freak fishing accident.

Book I: Bedroom Excuses

BONUS: FLOORDROBE EXCUSE

Welcome to my 'Floordrobe'...

...I know what you're thinking. It looks like I haven't tidied my room. But I can assure you that although it may look like a mess, it's actually a well organised mess.

BONUS: MISSING SOCK EXCUSE

Bedroom tidying has had to be paused...

... I've lost a sock! My current working theory is that my missing sock, the old TV remote and dad's shed key have banded together and fled to Mexico to start a new life together.

BONUS: MOORDEB EXCUSE

Did you know that bedroom spelt backwards is...

... Which in Dutch roughly translates to 'a child's sacred sanctuary void of all adult influence'. So, that's why I can't tidy my bedroom.

BONUS: HOLEY EXCUSE

Put my sock in the bin? No way . . .

. . . This sock is holey. It must be preserved for future generations.

Book 1: Bedroom Excuses

BONUS: YUMMA YUM BIRD EXCUSE

I can't tidy my bedroom because, look . . .

. . . The endangered Yumma Yum Bird has made it's nest in my pile of dirty clothes. Trust me, you don't want to mess with one of them!!! (For proof, read my book 'The Grotty Spoon').

BONUS: SOCK CARPET EXCUSE

I was bored of my old carpet . . .

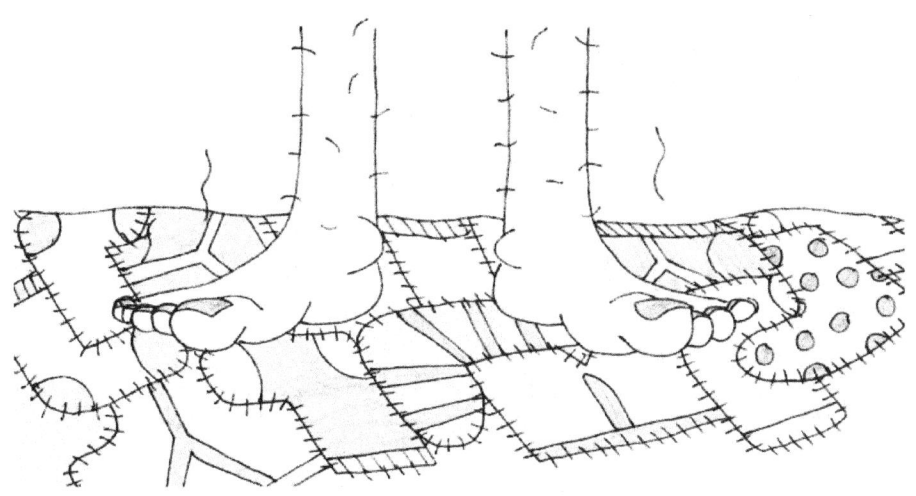

. . . So, instead of tidying my bedroom I've made a new carpet from all of the socks in my sock drawer (and also your sock drawer).

Book I: Bedroom Excuses

BONUS: HIDE AND SEEK EXCUSE

Shhhhhhhhhhhhhhhhh! . . .

. . . I'm in the finals of the Hide and Seek World Championships. I can't tidy my bedroom as this is my world-class hiding place. Wish me luck!

BONUS: SOCK CIRCLES EXCUSE

Don't. Move. Anything! . . .

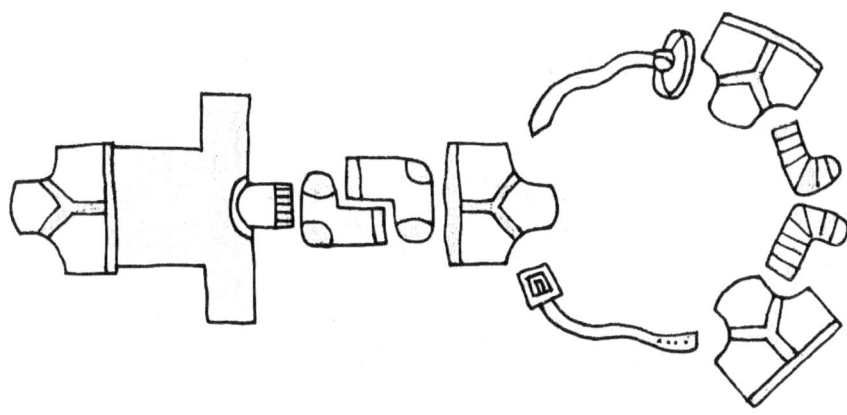

. . . Aliens have left us an important message, and they've done so using my dirty laundry on the floor of my bedroom. We shall call it a 'sock circle'.

Book I: Bedroom Excuses

BONUS: CHORE OF NATURE EXCUSE

As 'the child', it is my chore-of-nature to create mess...

...And as 'the parent', it is your chore-of-nature to tidy up. This is the circle of life that <u>MUST</u> be followed.

The Excuse Encyclopedia

BONUS: WILD WEST EXCUSE

I can't tidy my bedroom . . .

. . . The Sheriff has finally cornered Billy the Kid in this Wild West Saloon for a daring shootout (due to commence in ten days time).

Book 1: Bedroom Excuses

BONUS: THEIR MESS EXCUSE

But I've tidied up MY mess . . .

. . . You need to find the owners of this mess and get them to tidy it up.

BONUS: SOCK DRAWER DRAMA EXCUSE

I'll tidy my bedroom once I've caught up with my sock drawer drama...

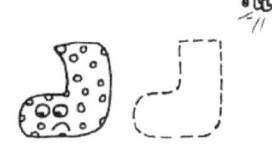

Ted is mourning the sudden disappearance of Julie (who has actually run away with Pablo to start a new life in Spain

Sally returned from the airing cupboard and has been reunited with Bob

Jeff left Mindy for Cindy

...As you can see, there is A LOT to gossip about today.

Book I: Bedroom Excuses

BONUS: ONLINE COURSE EXCUSE

I want to make sure I do the best job possible...

... To tidy my bedroom properly, first I must learn how. That's why I've just enrolled on a ten week intensive online course.

Ways to Steal the Cookie Jar

Book 2: Cookie Jar

1. BUY A TRAMPOLINE

I'm practising my Trampoline routine for the next Olympic Games . . .

. . . I know the kitchen isn't the best place to practise, but I honestly just picked this room at random.

2. STAND IN FERTILIZER

My science teacher taught me that plants grow faster in the sunshine, when they're well watered, and planted in fertilizer rich with nutrients . . .

. . . so this should speed up my growth spurt!

Book 2: Cookie Jar

3. CREATE THE MIRACLE COOKIE

After endless nights of research, I've discovered a cookie combination that produces a truly miraculous result . . .

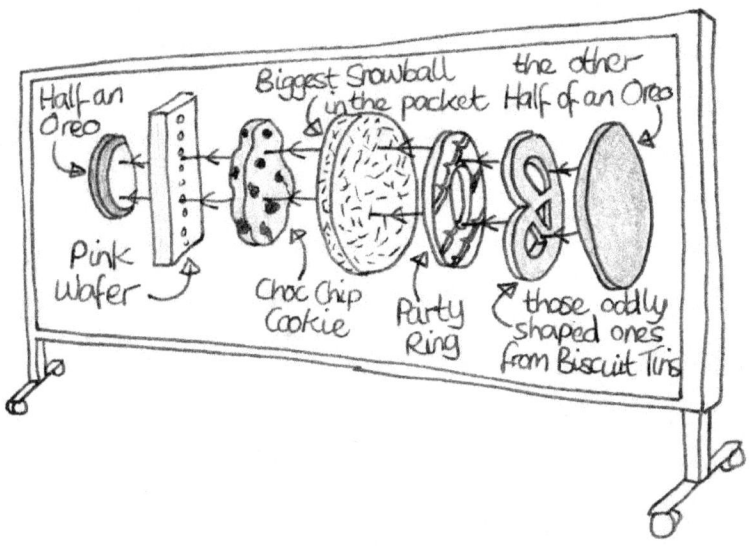

. . . one bite and you'll never be hungry again. As you can see, I've now finished the 'Theory Stage', so I'm going to need the Cookie Jar so I can begin the 'Testing Stage'.

The Excuse Encyclopedia

4. BIRD OF PREY

This is Robby, my pet budgie . . .

. . . he can smell a cookie from a mile away and his razor sharp claws can rip through metal. No matter where you hide the Cookie Jar, Robbie will find it, he will ferociously attack it, and I will have a cookie before bedtime!

5. THE COOKIE MAINTENANCE MAN

We received a call from a Mr. Rogers about a serious problem with his Cookie Jar...

... I'll happily take a look at it now. By the way, the callout charge is 2 Chocolate Bourbons, and the repair charges can range from a Jam Doughnut to a Double Fudge Chocolate Cake.

The Excuse Encyclopedia

6. THE THREE CUP TRICK

The cookie is under one of these three cups. Pick the right one and you'll win the cookie . . .

. . . Wow! I must have made the cookie disappear by magic! Did I mention it costs a cookie for every guess, which means you now owe me three cookies.

Book 2: Cookie Jar

7. HAND-DRAWN COOKIE WATCH

My new hand-drawn watch says it's Cookie o'clock in 3 minutes...

... and again in 18 minutes, in 33 minutes, in 48 minutes, and in 63 minutes too. So I'm going to need the Cookie Jar to keep up with my new watch!

8. AN IMPORTANT QUESTION

Can cookies bring you lasting happiness?

. . .

. . . give me the Cookie Jar and I will give you a comprehensive written answer in 2-3 hours.

9. TRAIN A CHIMP

This is my trainee Chimp, Boris...

... I'm training him to sneak into the kitchen, climb up the wall and steal the Cookie Jar. It's early days, but I think I'm making good progress.

The Excuse Encyclopedia

10. ASSEMBLE AN ELITE COOKIE SQUAD

Say hello to my Elite Squad of Deadly Cookie Snatchers...

...Cookie Squad, get me that Cookie Jar.

Book 2: Cookie Jar

11. BUILD A PET PYRAMID

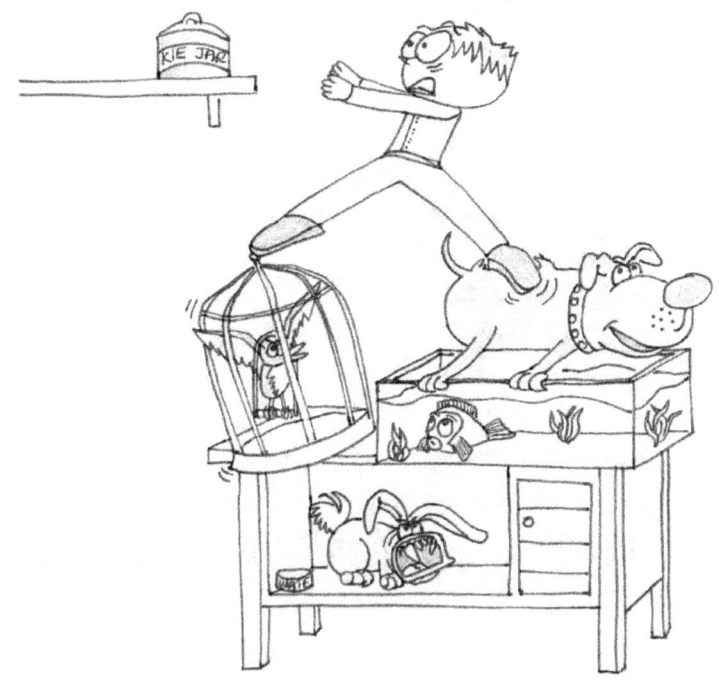

12. FAKE DOCTOR'S PHONE CALL

"Hello this is Katie . . ." *pause* "Good Afternoon Doctor, do you have the results from my tests . . .

. . . really, I have a Cookie-Deficiency. . ." *pause* "If I don't eat enough cookies I'll transform into a little monster and become a danger to society . . ." *pause* "And the treatment is to eat cookies until you can discover a cure . . ." *pause* "Okay, I'll pass on the information to my parents and thank you Doctor."

13. CHARITY APPEAL

Our school is raising money for charity. All my friends are doing the normal stuff -- sponsored fun runs, sponsored bike rides, sponsored silence. So I've decided to do something completely different...

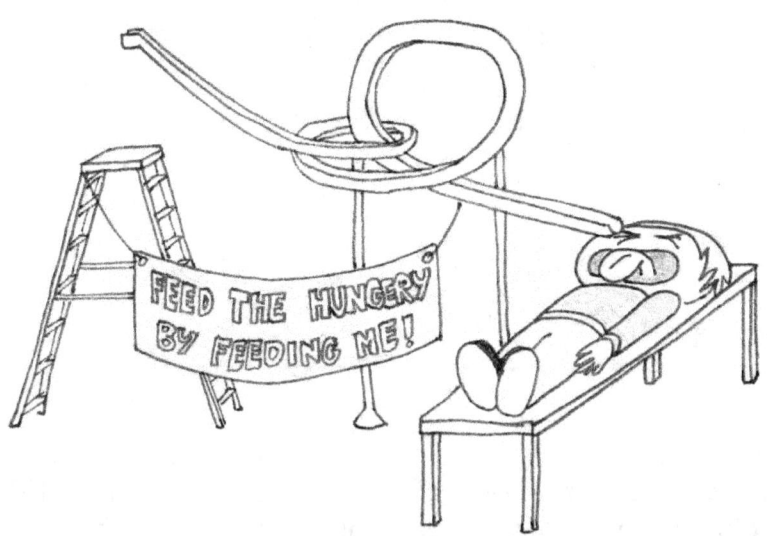

... I'm going to do a sponsored Cookie-a-thon. My target is to raise $10,000 by eating 10,000 cookies. Would you like to be the first person to sponsor me?

14. BEWARE THE CROCOSECT!

Oh no! A plague of Crocosects are coming down our street. What? You've never heard of a Crocosect? . . .

. . . they've got the head of a Crocodile, the body of an insect, and the appetite of a teenage boy! Pass me the Cookie Jar and I'll hide it under my pillow, then you grab the fruit bowl and hide it under my little brother's pillow.

15. GROW YOUR FINGERNAILS

What's that Mum? Why am I growing my finger nails? . . .

. . . no particular reason. Haven't you got some ironing to do?

16. THE PIPE PIPER

I bought this tin whistle and it seems to work wonders on the rats...

...if only they liked Custard Creams more than Mini Cheddars!

Book 2: Cookie Jar

17. WRITE A LETTER

I know how to unite the world in peace and love . . .

. . . all we need to do is share our cookies. For the best results I suggest Jammie Dodgers.

The Excuse Encyclopedia

18. WINGARDIUM LEVIOSA

For my home-made wand I've used hair from the tail of the neighbour's dog as the core and a 7 and ½ inch twig from the garden...

... Hermione makes the Levitation Charm look much easier in the films!

19. MONSTER ATTACK

Mum, mum, the Cookie Monster smashed through the TV Screen...

... quick, hand me the Cookie Jar and I'll run to my room, jam a chair under the handle, and keep our Cookie Jar safe from that blue, fuzzy monster.

20. THE HOLY RECIPE

I've spent the last few months studying at the Sacred Monastery on the peak of Crumble Mountain . . .

. . . I have studied the Ancient Scrolls passed down by 'The Ancestors' from generation to generation. They contain the holy recipe for the perfect batch of cookies. According to my translation, they may only be prepared and baked by a loving mother and eaten by her most worthy son.

21. LEARN MARTIAL ARTS

Be warned, I've mastered Karate...

... I can karate chop through eight Bourbons, karate kick through fourteen Chocolate Fingers and face slam through a Jammy Wagon Wheelie. So don't mess with me! Now hand over the Cookie Jar and no harm shall come to your or your cookies.

22. USE ANCIENT WAR TACTICS

I tried using ancient war tactics I learned in last week's History lesson . . .

. . . but I'm guessing the Trojans didn't conquer a Kingdom on an empty stomach.

23. CHAMELEON MAN

The chameleon has solved the 'Cookie Jar' problem with the combination of camouflage, suction pads, and a sticky extendable tongue...

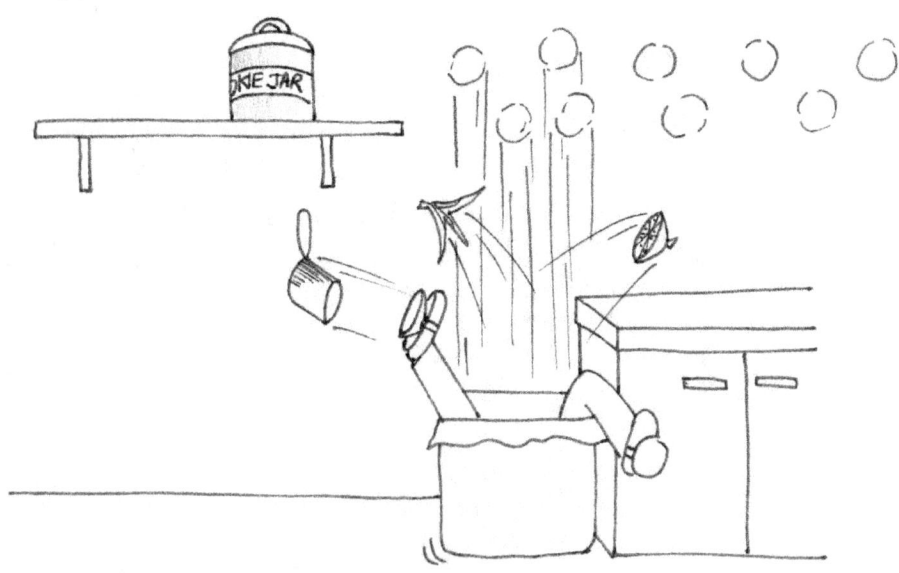

... should have tried the camouflage. Darn slippy kitchen tiles!

24. CREATE AN AMAZING INVENTION

I think I've cracked the world's energy crisis with my amazing invention -- The Crumble-nator...

... it runs on cookie crumbs by sweeping them up and churns them into pure energy. It's only in the experimental phase, so for the good of all humanity and the environment I'm going to need the Cookie Jar.

Book 2: Cookie Jar

25. TRY A GIANT ELECTRO-MAGNET

26. VISIT FROM THE COOKIE INSPECTOR

Good morning Sir. I'm with the Government's Special Branch for the National Cookie Inspection. My colleagues will be here shortly to do the measure, sniff, weight, and crumble tests. I'm here to do the 'Taste Test'. . .

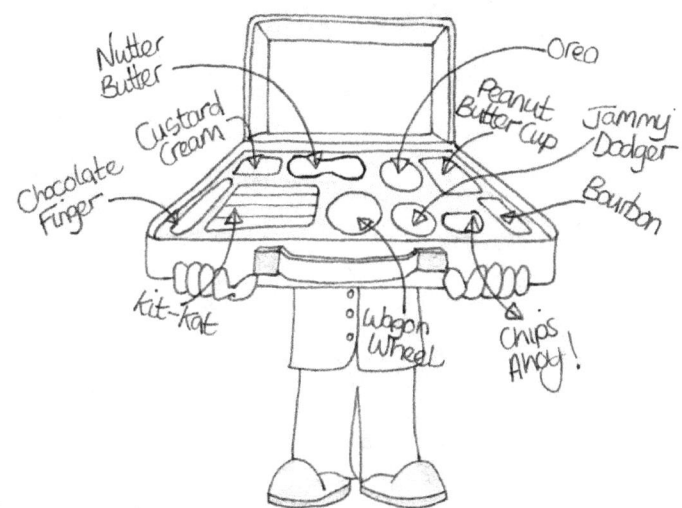

. . . I'm going to need a sample of every type of Cookie in your house. Then I'll take them back to our Government Labs for testing and send your results in the post. By the way, the 'Poor Cookie Quality Fine' is $1,000. Good luck!

27. DO ALIENS LIKE COOKIES?

For this week's homework I've got to write an essay on one of life's BIG questions. I'm going to tackle a big one -- if aliens exist which cookie would be their favourite? ...

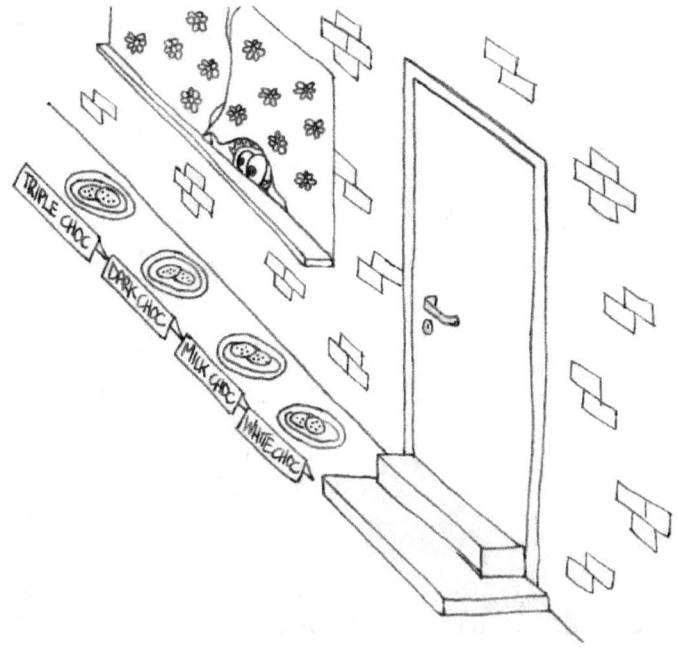

... I'm going to leave out different cookies and see which ones are still here in the morning.

28. BORROW YOUR DAD'S FISHING ROD

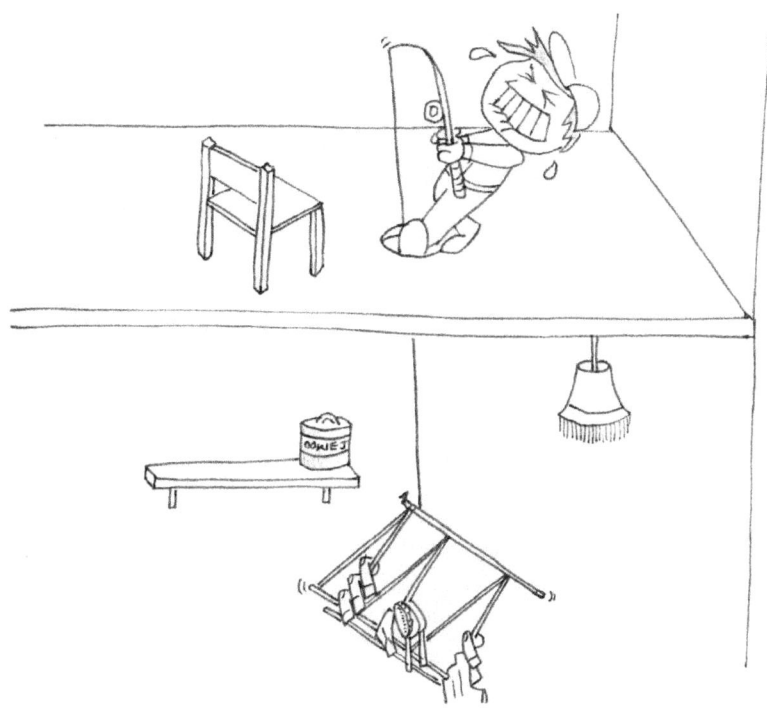

29. RESIZE & REDISTRIBUTE

I've decided that our family Cookie Jar should be split between each member . . .

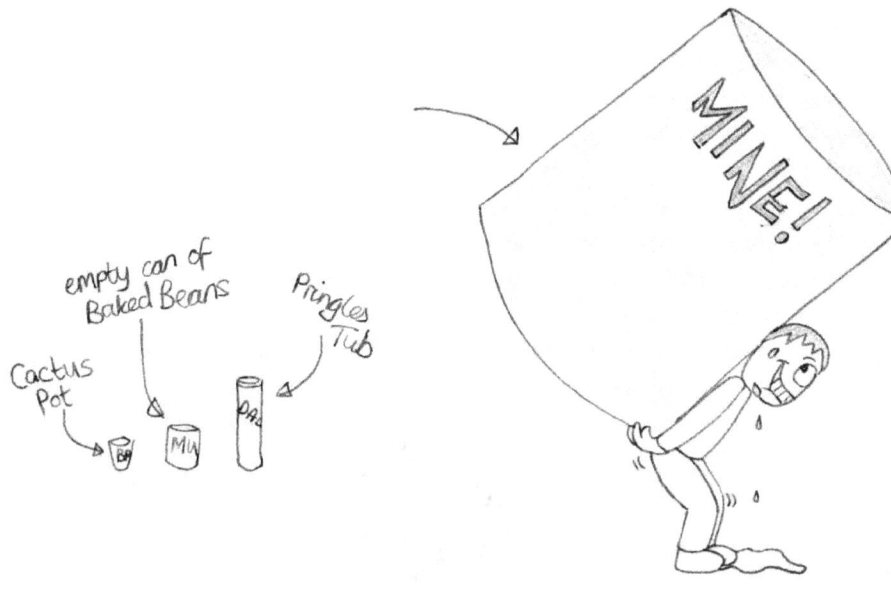

. . . I took many factors into account - average daily consumption, height to weight ratio, and who currently has the highest score on Angry Birds. According to my data analysis, these are our new Cookie Jars. Due to its size I think mine should live in my bedroom.

30. LEARN THE TARZAN SWING

Tarzan would use a Jungle Vine to swing to his target. You won't find any Jungle Vines in the kitchen so I'm using the washing line. and there aren't many solid wood kitchen tables in the Jungle either.

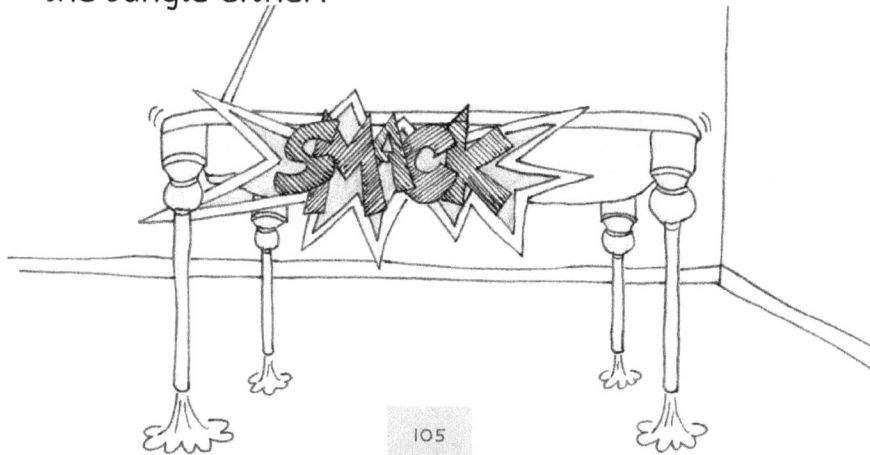

31. BRING IN THE LAWYERS

I didn't want it to come to this but you leave me no choice. This is my team of brilliantly-minded, ruthlessly-cunning Lawyers . . .

. . . they've been building a damning legal case against you -- parental corruption, bribery, blackmail, and organised child slavery. But it'll all go away if you sign over the 'Ownership Contract' of the Cookie Jar to me! It's that simple.

The Excuse Encyclopedia

32. NEED SOME GRANDMA BAIT

Dad, I'm going fishing for another Grandma...

... it's a well-known fact the best bait for Grandma's is shortbread. I'll catch a good one, have a cup of tea and some shortbread with her, and then bring home my prize winning catch. Would you pass me the Cookie Jar, I mean the Bait Box?

Book 2: Cookie Jar

33. HOME-MADE SECURITY VAULT

Have you heard the news? Cookie Crime is up by over 500% in our neighbourhood! . . .

. . . but there's no need to panic. I'll happily keep them in my Home-Made Security Vault for safe keeping.

The Excuse Encyclopedia

34. THE DECEASED COOKIE JAR

Dad, I have some bad news. While you were out washing the car the Cookie Jar had a massive heart attack and passed away...

... we held a short, touching funeral in the kitchen and then I found the perfect place to bury him.

35. THE 3 RULES OF CHILDHOOD

The three most important rules in childhood: 1) Eat cookies. 2) Give your daughter what she wants all the time. 3) . . .

. . . erm, sorry I've forgotten the last one. Why is my hand still empty?

The Excuse Encyclopedia

36. WHAT WOULD ROBIN HOOD DO?

I've decided to adopt the Robin Hood philosophy...

... take from the rich (the Cookie Jar), and give to the poor (my empty stomach).

37. BECOME AN AUTHOR

I've spent the past 6 years of my life researching the nutritional benefits of the Hobnob . . .

. . . my ground-breaking research suggests they have all the nutrients required for everlasting health, happiness, and handsomeness. Here, have a free copy of my bestselling book – 'Hobnobs: The Elixir of Life'.

38. LEARN HYPNOSIS

Look deep into my eyes . . .

. . . empty the contents of the Cookie Jar on my dinner plate. Then cook Spinach & Broccoli Soup for my little brother. And every time he says 'I hate my sister', fill his school lunch box with raw Brussels Sprouts.

39. BECOME THE SHOPPING TROLLEY GHOST!

40. EXTERMINATE THE COOKIES

Our nation is suffering from a terrible infestation - Cookie Termites!! . . .

. . . I know this sounds extreme, but the only way to get rid of them is to eat every single cookie on the planet. Cut off their food supply and we'll kill the vermin! My belly is empty so I'll happily begin the extermination with our Cookie Jar.

Book 2: Cookie Jar

41. READ FROM THE BIBLE

Today's reading will be from Genesis 1:42-43 . . .

. . . "And on the 8th day God created cookies, and declared it to be the food of humankind. For the heavenly snack contained everything they needed to live: peace, love, and plenty of chocolate chips." Now let us praise God by opening his sacred Cookie Jar and enjoying his scrumptious creation.

42. INSTALL A COOKIE-METER

Stop right there sir, this is now a 'Parking Meter Zone' . . .

. . . you've got to pay using this Cookie Meter: 1 Chocolate Chip Cookie for 1 hour, 1 Double Chocolate Chip Cookie for 2 hours, or 1 Triple Chocolate Chip Cookie for 3 hours or more.

43. BECOME A NUTRITIONIST

I decided that when I grow up I'd like to become a Nutritionist...

... the great thing about being a Nutritionist is you get to decide what you eat. Here's this week's meal list for me and my little brother.

44. THE MOUSE TRAP

DAD!!! COME QUICK!!! THERE'S A MOUSE IN THE COOKIE JAR! . . .

. . . relax Dad, this was just a test of your response time in saving our family's most precious and valued possession. Congratulations, you passed, which means I honour you with the prestigious title 'Protector of the Cookie Jar'. Your next test will measure how much you love your daughter (hint, hint).

45. OFFER TO DO THE DUSTING

I know how busy you are with work, housework, and parenting me. So I've decided I'd give you a helping hand by doing the dusting . . .

. . . I'm starting with the spider's web in the corner above the Cookie Jar.

46. CONSTRUCTION SITE

I'm attempting a world record in Cookie Packaging Construction...

...the highest building made entirely out of empty boxes of cookies! I'm so close to the record, all I need is an extra couple of inches. Help me make history by passing me the Cookie Jar.

Book 2: Cookie Jar

47. ACQUIRE THE RAW INGREDIENTS

Mum, I need some items for this week's homework: butter, sugar, flour, eggs, chocolate chips, and a bowl . . .

. . . I need the butter to make a butter sculpture for my Art homework, sugar to help me count to a thousand for my Maths homework, flour to use as make-up for my Mime performance in Drama, eggs to practise my juggling skills for my Gym homework, chocolate chips for my lunchbox, and a bowl to use as a helmet in our World War II reconstruction in History Class.

48. DISSECTION LESSON

I forgot to tell you last night, we're dissecting a penguin in Science Class tomorrow . . .

. . . don't look so horrified. The chocolate-coated cookie, not the Antarctic-waddling animal. I also forgot to tell you that Mark, Robby, Dean, Chloe, Tanya, George, and Violet are all cookie-tarians* so I said I'd bring them a penguin to dissect from our Cookie Jar.

* Cookie-tarian: someone who refuses to eat any cookie-dough based food due to cruelty to butter.

49. ASK POLITELY

Still no cookie? Why not try asking politely.

". . . go on. If the other 48 ways haven't worked, it's worth a go!"

The Excuse Encyclopedia

BONUS: RAID THE SHOE RACK

Why am I wearing all the shoes in the house? . . .

. . . No reason!

BONUS: MINECRAFT DAD

If you give me a cookie, I'll create a Minecraft version of you . . .

. . . WITH HAIR! (Caution: this will only work if your dad is bald and likes Minecraft).

BONUS: COOKIES CHALLENGE

Have you ever wondered what would happen if someone ate all the cookies in the cookie jar . . .

. . . I have. Want to find out?

Book 2: Cookie Jar

BONUS: BORING CONVERSATION

Thanks for the lovely conversation . . .

. . . I do hope you'll find something new to complain about next time while I pretend to listen and eat the entire packet of cookies.

BONUS: CHANGE THE EXPIRATION DATE

It says on the cookie dough packaging that the expiration date is TODAY...

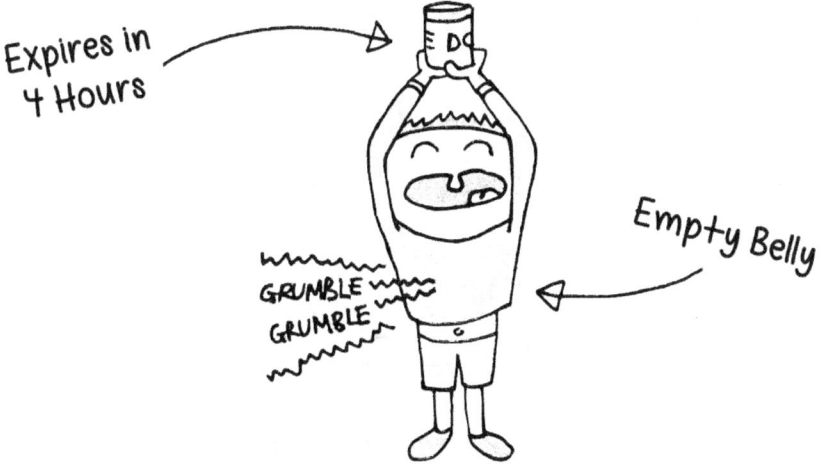

... Quick. Put the oven on and bake it so that it doesn't go to waste. I'll take one for the team and eat them as soon as they cool down.

Book 2: Cookie Jar

BONUS: UNRESTRICTED ACCESS

Do you know what would totally help you gain my respect? . . .

. . . These two magic words in regards to the cookie jar.

The Excuse Encyclopedia

BONUS: SHORTBREAD FOR SHORT PEOPLE

After months of tireless campaign I've finally been able to change the law . . .

. . . It is now illegal for tall people to eat shortbread. You tall people can keep your Brandy Snaps and Chocolate Fingers, but hand over all your shortbread or I'll call the police.

Book 2: Cookie Jar

BONUS: BANANA TORTURE

Stick em' up . . .

. . . Hand over the cookie jar or the banana gets it!

BONUS: STOCKPILE COOKIE CUTTERS

SURPRISE!!! . . .

. . . I've bought you some brand new cookie cutters. You better hurry up and give them all a go right away.

Book 2: Cookie Jar

BONUS: SIX COOKIES

Did you know that you are five times more likely to give me a cookie than win the lottery?
. . .

. . . So, give me six cookies and then go buy yourself a lottery ticket.

The Excuse Encyclopedia

BONUS: MAKE A CUPPA

I've made you this delicious cuppa tea . . .

Delicious Cuppa Tea

. . . So, I'd recommend that you get the cookie jar down immediately and leave it at eye level while you go put your feet up and relax for the next ten to twenty minutes.

Book 2: Cookie Jar

BONUS: STRIKE A DEAL

You've got something I want and I've got something you want . . .

. . . I want cookies and you want some peace and quiet. So, sit down and let's start drafting a deal.

BOOK THREE

Excuses for Not Doing Your Homework

HOMEWORK EXCUSES

Book 3: Homework Excuses

1. THE MIX-UP EXCUSE

What? You're collecting *Maths* homework this morning? But I did the *Reading* homework . . .

. . . Oh I know what's happened. I've accidentally mixed-up my maths homework with my little sisters homework to read 'The Hungry Caterpillar'. I hope little Suzie didn't struggle with those algebraic equations.

2. THE NEWLY QUALIFIED EXCUSE

I signed up to a *'Fast Track Teacher Training Course'* over the weekend . . .

. . . my Teaching Certificate, accredited by *UniversityForDummies.com,* came through the post this morning and I got a Distinction! So if you'd care to take a seat I'll take it from here Miss.

3. THE NASA EXCUSE

My application to the *'NASA Young Astronauts Program'* has come back. I've been accepted . . .

. . . From now on my homework is set by the NASA Officials. My homework this week is to: eat a mars bar everyday, practice my zero gravity walk, and learn how to countdown from 10 in a deep and dramatic voice.

The Excuse Encyclopedia

4. THE ALIEN SPA EXCUSE

You'll never guess what happened to me last night . . .

. . . I was abducted by Aliens! They took me to their Spa Therapy Spaceship and gave me an *'Intergalactic Mud Bath'*, *'Slug Slime Facial'*, and an *'Asteroid Field Massage'*. It was so cool that I signed you up as their next applicant. Hope you have a relaxing evening Miss.

Book 3: Homework Excuses

5. THE HAMSTER-NAPPED EXCUSE

I was about to do my homework last night, when I found this Ransom Note in my Maths Book...

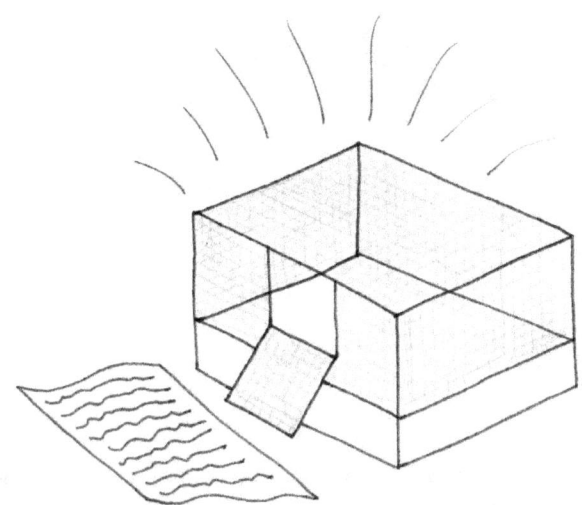

... Someone's hamster-napped Hammy the Class Hamster! They want all our dinner money and absolutely no homework for a whole week. I think you'll agree it's our only option!

6. THE GENIUS EXCUSE

Did you hear about the kid who has a higher IQ than Albert Einstein? . . .

. . . That's me. I'll be setting all the homework from now on, and try to keep up Miss.

Book 3: Homework Excuses

7. THE BAD HEARING EXCUSE

Oh no! I must have misheard you . . .

. . . I thought you said 'don't forget your English home *jerk*'. I drew this picture of William Shakespeare with goofy glasses because Macbeth goes on for far too long without any cool explosions or car chases!

The Excuse Encyclopedia

8. THE COPYRIGHT EXCUSE

Big news everyone. I've bought the copyright to the word *'Homework'*...

... From now on no-one is allowed to say, write, print, or even whisper MY WORD without my prior permission. You were saying Miss... something about me forgetting to do something?

9. THE HEAD-START EXCUSE

I got bored of all the *easy* homework you've been setting lately . . .

. . . So I decided to write a book over the weekend. I'm going to call it *'Jenny's Dictionary'*. It contains every single word in the English language, spelt correctly of course. Consider this masterpiece my English homework for the rest of the year.

The Excuse Encyclopedia

10. THE FORWARD PLANNING EXCUSE

I'm getting tired of making up excuses each week for why I forgot my homework...

... So I decided to spend all night writing a long list of brilliant excuses. Just pick one each week and I'll shrug my shoulders and grin cheekily.

Book 3: Homework Excuses

11. THE SUPPLY TEACHER EXCUSE

Miss Print, you're not supposed to be teaching your class today. You've got the day off . . .

. . . You've been selected at random to represent the National Teacher Association at *Disney Land's 'Education Day'*. I'll be taking your class, now run along your plane leaves in 20 minutes.

12. THE NEW CALENDAR EXCUSE

Haven't you heard, the Government have introduced a brand new Calendar...

ALL-NEW CALENDAR						
SAT1	SAT2	SUN1	SUN2	MON	SAT3	SUN3
28	29	30	31	1	2	3
4	5	6	7	8	9	10
11	12	13	14	15	16	17
18	19	20	21	22	23	24
25	26	27	28	29	30	1

... As you can see we've got a busy week ahead. Plus according to the new calendar today isn't Monday, instead it's Saturday, so I'm going back to bed.

Book 3: Homework Excuses

13. THE S.B.F. EXCUSE

Timmy's brain has gone on vacation due to S.B.F. Disease (Severe Brain Freeze)...

... his brain has gone to the Bahamas to thaw off on the beach. Do not set him any homework until his brain has returned (unless the homework is to drool on a piece of paper).

14. THE POWERPOINT EXCUSE

I have forgotten my homework, but I have several excellent excuses . . .

. . . please take a seat and I'll show the PowerPoint Presentation I've prepared demonstrating my forgetfulness but positive attitude for the Education System.

Book 3: Homework Excuses

15. THE HORRIFIC ACCIDENT EXCUSE

I was in a Paper-Round Accident over the summer holiday and broke both my arms . . .

. . . there's a new Super-Computer I could use to do my homework that works through blinking, telepathy and tongue movements. So unless the school can pay for it I can't do any homework for the next 6 months... Did I mention it costs $500,000?

16. THE HOMELESS EXCUSE

I couldn't do my homework last night because I no longer have a home . . . I'm homeless . . .

. . . If it was called *'pavement-outside-of-the-local-shop-work'* I would have done it, but it's called *'homework'* so naturally it doesn't apply to me!

17. THE ALPHABET EXCUSE

I've realised over the weekend that someone needs to put your teaching skills to question...

... can we, your class of up-and-coming masterminds, trust you to set our homework when the alphabet poster in your classroom is clearly wrong!

18. THE BACK-WORDS EXCUSE

!sdrawkcab kaeps ylno nac I won dna gnorw ylbirroh tnew tnemirepxe ecneics edam-emoh yM . . .

Book 3: Homework Excuses

19. THE SCIENCE SHOW-DOWN EXCUSE

I told my good friend and mentor that you think you're the best science teacher in the world, so now he has challenged you to a Science-Off...

...Mr Steven Hawkins said you shouldn't bother setting homework tonight seeing as this pile of books is your revision for the show-down tomorrow. Good luck Miss.

20. THE DISEASED EXCUSE

I've got some bad news Miss. I've been diagnosed with Brain & Hand Disease...

... it's a strain of Foot & Mouth Disease, which means that my brain no longer has control of my arms! They've been wiggling and wobbling like this all weekend. My homework is just one big squiggle.

Book 3: Homework Excuses

21. THE STUDENT BECOMES THE TEACHER EXCUSE

I believe we, as your students, would learn more if our roles were reversed...

... and if you don't like what I have to say then sit down and shut up or I will report you to the Headteacher. Now then class, this mornings lesson is a field trip to McDonald's.

The Excuse Encyclopedia

22. THE HOMEWORK BUDDY EXCUSE

You've never heard of a Homework Buddy ...

... Well Miss, they're like a Pen Pal except instead of simply writing letters you also swap homework. My Homework Buddy, Abu from Peru, is currently doing my homework and I'm doing his. I've got to knit a blanket out of Llama Wool.

23. EDUCATION CONSPIRACY EXCUSE

I've been working on a conspiracy theory. We're not in school to colour in, and cut and stick, and play in the playground . . . are we? . . .

. . . you're moulding us into responsible adults that will contribute to our modern society through taking jobs, and paying taxes, and being good citizens. Be warned, I'm on to you!

24. THE LOST IT! EXCUSE

Have you heard of the Bermuda Triangle Miss . . .

. . . in the North Atlantic Ocean . . . dangerous waters . . . infamous for paranormal activity . . . Well I accidentally dropped my homework in it on the way to school and a sea monster ate it.

Book 3: Homework Excuses

25. THE INSANITY EXCUSE

Why did I forget to bring my homework and why am I wearing underpants on my head? . . .

. . . Well Miss, I've recently moved house to the Mental Asylum. This is how my new friends wear underpants. By the way, my doctor says that my new homework is to stop chewing my elbow.

26. THE EXTERNAL HELP EXCUSE

Please forward all homework to: derek@domyhomeworkforme.com

Book 3: Homework Excuses

27. THE 'PRIEST OF THE LAZY WAY' EXCUSE

Now that I have said my Holy Vows I can no longer partake in this worldly activity you call *'homework'*...

... as a *Priest of the Lazy Way* I must set an example to the world by devoting my entire life to doing nothing. Thank you for your support in advance.

28. THE MARATHON EXCUSE

My homework is ruined! . . .

. . . I shouldn't have stored my homework in my shoe and then completed a marathon before school.

29. THE SHORTCUT EXCUSE

My homework is ruined! . . .

. . . that's the last time I take a shortcut to school through the zoo when the Elephants have got a cold!

30. THE LIFT TO SCHOOL EXCUSE

My homework is ruined! . . .

. . . that's the last time I ask my Uncle Roy for a lift. He is a part-time Snake Charmer, part-time Yo-Yo Mechanic, part-time Skydiving Instructor.

Book 3: Homework Excuses

31. THE SHORTCUT EXCUSE CONT.

My homework is ruined! . . .

. . . that's the last time I take a shortcut to school through the fire swamp.

32. THE CLASSIC (WITH A TWIST) EXCUSE

What happened to your homework this week Harry? Did your dog eat it again? . . .

. . . actually my pet goldfish ate my homework, who was eaten by the neighbour's cat, who was eaten by my pet dog. It would be a painstakingly complex surgical procedure to retrieve my homework so let's assume I got all the questions right.

33. PSYCHOPATHIC PENCIL CASE EXCUSE

You have got to help me Miss! My pencil case is trying to kill me! . . .

. . . it might look innocent but it's plotting something evil.

34. THE STOLEN EXCUSE

Do you know the girl with cute little pigtails, inch thick glasses, always knows the answer to every single question...

... she stole my homework. You want proof? Just look at the homework. If all the answers are correct then it's definitely mine.

35. THE TALENTLESS EXCUSE

I regret to inform you that I cannot do my homework anymore. I am working on my America's Got Talent act . . .

. . . 'The Talentless Kid'. My sister has pushed me around in this cart all summer so that I haven't had to lift a finger. I'm going to become the very first person to become famous for doing absolutely nothing!

36. THE HAIRDRESSING EXCUSE

Oh dear! I must have misheard the homework. I thought you said 'don't forget your *comb*work' . . .

. . . this fabulous hair-do took 3 hours of none-stop-combing and three tins of super-strong hairspray.

37. THE INACCURATE QUESTION EXCUSE

The Maths question you set yesterday is extremely flawed . . .

. . . I went to the train station and took the New York to Washington D.C. train and it took 5 hours and 38 minutes, instead of 2 hours as the question clearly stated. Oh, and you also owe me $85 for the train ticket.

38. THE MY PET CALLED... EXCUSE

I didn't forget my homework. Look . . .

. . . this is my adorable pet dog called *Homework*. She needs constant attention, regular walks to the park and a T-Bone Steak every hour. Otherwise she'll become dangerously aggressive and eat all the chairs!

Book 3: Homework Excuses

39. THE SHORTCUT EXCUSE CONT.

My homework is ruined! . . .

. . . that's the last time I'll take the shortcut over the lake using my homemade jetpack.

40. THE LIFT TO SCHOOL EXCUSE CONT.

My homework is ruined! . . .

. . . that's the last time I'll be asking this guy for a lift!

Book 3: Homework Excuses

41. THE FORGETFUL EXCUSE

I'm sorry Miss, I forgot my homework . . .

. . . you want to hear an excuse? Oh darn it I forgot that too! It took 2 hours to come up with the perfect excuse . . . if only some author would write a book full of brilliant excuses!

42. THE SQUARE EYES EXCUSE

I never thought it would happen, but it did. My eyes have gone square! . . .

. . . Here's a note from my Optician explaining that from now on my eyes can only see screens. So until the school buys me an iPad I can't do my homework.

43. THE CHARITABLE EXCUSE

I didn't have time to do my homework this weekend because I've been doing charity work non-stop...

... I cooked and served tomato soup for the homeless in the morning, then I ran the London Marathon as a dolphin, then I wrote a pop song for charity with Bono, and then I helped Mrs. Doris across the road. Quite honestly Miss I think I deserve the morning off!

44. THE PRACTISING EXCUSE

What? You didn't say 'don't forget your gnomework?' . . .

. . . but I've watched Snow White and the Seven Dwarfs on repeat all weekend. Plus I've learnt all the words to the song 'Hi-Ho, Hi-Ho'.

45. THE BIRTHDAY EXCUSE

What . . . your birthday is next month . . .

. . . you mean you're telling me I've been hiding in this present all *weekend* waiting to surprise you, and in doing so missed the homework deadline, when it's not your birthday!

46. THE PLAYGROUND ILLNESS EXCUSE

I am terribly sorry to inform you that over the weekend I've become dangerously allergic to... *everyone*...

...When I touch another person they freeze to the spot. I discovered my awful condition when I was playing tag in the playground. Unfortunately I couldn't do my homework because I am the homework for hundreds of scientists while they research a cure.

Book 3: Homework Excuses

47. THE DEMOTED EXCUSE

Did you not get the memo, you've been demoted to Teaching Assistant...

... Let me introduce you to our new class teacher Mr. Google. We ask a question, you type it and Mr. Google gives us the answer. Simple!

48. THE POETRY EXCUSE

I know I forgot my homework again, so instead I wrote you a lovely poem as an apology . . .

. . . and if you are setting English homework this week my poem so counts!

49. THE HONEST EXCUSE

Well Miss, in truth I forgot it. Sorry . . .

. . . but I understand why I should do my homework:

1. To improve my intelligence, memory and problem solving skills
2. To keep a positive attitude towards study
3. To learn how to manage my time and work independently
4. To communicate better with my parents
5. To mature into a well-rounded, quick-thinking, high-earning, tax-paying human being.

[Pause, smile sweetly and engage puppy dog eyes] So I promise I'll try harder next time and make you, my parents and myself proud.

The Excuse Encyclopedia

BONUS: HAND ILLNESS(ES) EXCUSE

I tried to do my homework but . . .

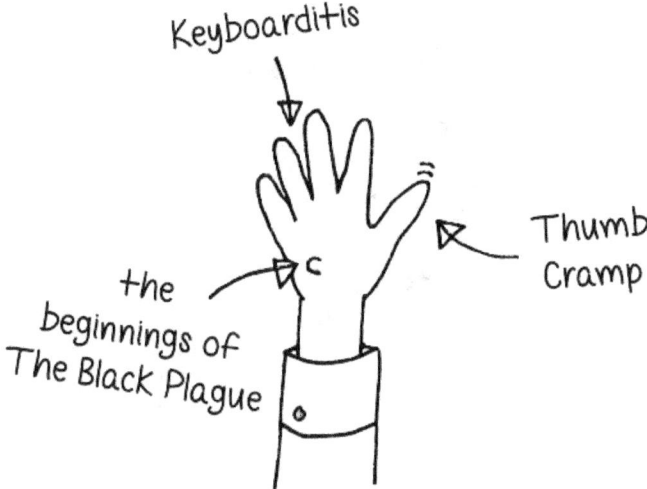

. . . my hand has been struck down by several deadly illnesses.

BONUS: THESAURUS EXCUSE

I've done my English homework for the rest of my school life...

...I call it the 'Thesaurus'. All the words for all my essays are inside, you'll just have to rearrange them to make the essays yourself.

BONUS: "I" BEFORE "E" EXCUSE

I'll happily do my English homework...

Weird policies, such as this, are neither scientific or neighbourly and should be reissued to banish the ancient rule forever

...once someone has finally sorted out that annoying 'i before e' rule... IT DOESN'T WORK!

Book 3: Homework Excuses

BONUS: WHAT DOESN'T KILL YOU EXCUSE

I know I forgot my homework today...

...but my dad always says 'what doesn't kill you makes you stronger' (and will probably make you write a really really long Facebook post).

BONUS: COCKY KID EXCUSE

The homework was too easy...

...However, you've become a much better teacher in my eyes. This is mainly because I've lowered my expectations.

Book 3: Homework Excuses

BONUS: SILLY FACT EXCUSE

Did you know that 70% of women use gas & air during child birth (and 99.9% of men have a cheeky whiff) . . .

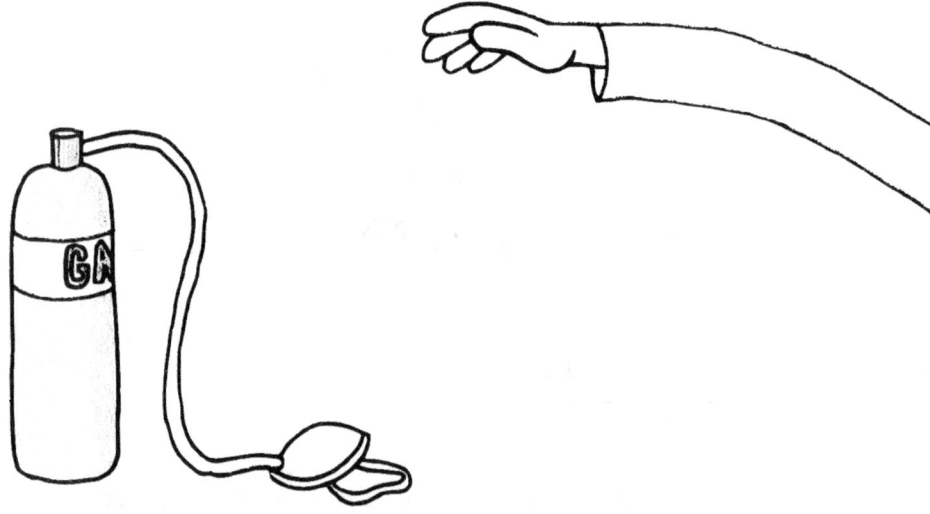

. . . What? The homework was not 'bring a silly fact to school'?

BONUS: AMNESIA EXCUSE

Erm, hi. My doctor says I have amnesia . .

. . . Are you my teacher? Is this my classroom? What's homework?

Book 3: Homework Excuses

BONUS: BRAIN SURGERY EXCUSE

Don't worry, Sir. I've had experimental brain surgery...

...There's no point in training this one as I've now got Albert Einstein's.

BONUS: ESSAY EXCUSE

Would you like to read my essay . . .

. . . great, but first you will need to write it and then you can enjoy reading it.

Book 3: Homework Excuses

BONUS: HEAVEN COLLEGE EXCUSE

This is my last day at this dead-beat school...

... I'll be going to a new school that doesn't believe in homework. It's called Heaven College. That's right, I've got a scholarship to become an angel.

BONUS: SCHOOL/ LIFE BALANCE EXCUSE

School is for work and home is for play . .

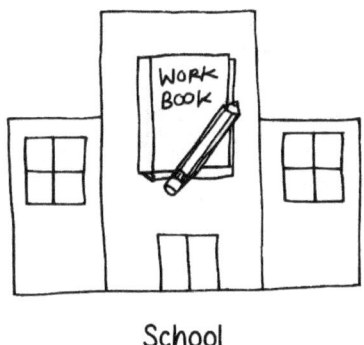
School

Home

. . . END OF DISCUSSION!

Book 3: Homework Excuses

BONUS: SATURDAY PART-ONE EXCUSE

 You've can't set any homework today, Sir

. . . Why? Because today isn't Friday, I've renamed it Saturday Part-One. I no longer believe that 'Fridays' exist. So, I need you to respect my beliefs by sending me home so I can start the weekend.

The Excuse Encyclopedia

BONUS: TIGER EXCUSE

A tiger ate my homework...

...You know, the one who came for tea.

BOOK FOUR

Questions to Annoy Your Parents

1. THE SHOES QUESTION

You know when you said *they've got a tough life, you should try walking in their shoes* . . .

. . . I'm wearing their shoes now and I've been walking for miles. I still don't understand their hardships, in fact I think I've just made it worse by stealing their shoes.

2. THE VAMPIRE QUESTION

Would a Jewish Vampire cower at the sight of a Christian cross? . . .

. . . because if not I will start carrying around a symbol for every major world religion, just in case I'm attacked by a spiritually curious vampire.

3. THE FRUIT & VEG QUESTION

My teacher told me that I should eat five portions of fruit and veg every day . . .

. . . do strawberry laces, orange lollipops, and Jaffa Cakes count?.

4. THE SNAIL QUESTION

Is what Douglas said in the playground true? . . .

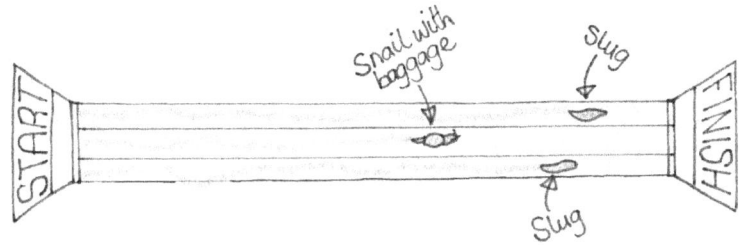

. . . he said that snails are actually slugs with baggage. That's why they go slightly slower in a race.

Book 4: Annoying Questions

5. THE ATLAS QUESTION

Who drew the dotted lines around the countries? . . .

. . . they must have used a huge pen!

6. THE HOT DRINKS QUESTION

Why do adults drink so much tea & coffee?
. . .

. . . does it make you more intelligent? Is it a cure for some horrible terminal illness called 'aging'? It's peer pressure from your work colleagues, isn't it?

7. THE P.U. QUESTION

What does P.U. stand for, as in when someone says 'P.U. that stinks!' ...

... I have a few suggestions: Public Urinal, Prehistoric Underarms, Professional Uranus-ologist, Purple Umbrella.

The Excuse Encyclopedia

8. THE GOD QUESTION

Can God tie a knot that he can't undo? . .

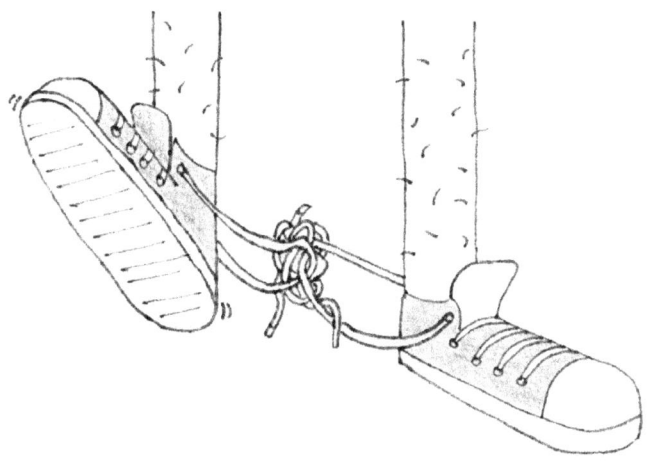

. . . because if so I'll stop praying for help untying my shoelaces and grab the scissors.

9. THE SIGN MAKER QUESTION

If sign makers were to go on strike and protest up and down the street...

...would they have to carry blank boards and empty placards?

The Excuse Encyclopedia

10. THE BABIES QUESTION

I know all about where babies come from, daddies put them in mummies tummies. But I still have some extra questions . . .

. . . where were they before that? Do they live in heaven? Or the zoo? Or maybe Lapland? How do they get here? Who looks after them all?

Book 4: Annoying Questions

11. THE UNDERWATER QUESTION

Can you cry underwater? . . .

. . . also can you juggle, knit, play the trumpet, or do a crossword underwater?

The Excuse Encyclopedia

12. THE BAKED BEAN QUESTION

How does this tiny little baked bean turn into a loud . . .

. . . you know . . . rude, but funny noise?

13. THE PARKING QUESTION

Why do adults complain about parking so much? . . .

. . . I'm thinking of starting a business called 'The Easy Parking Rental Company'. As you're my parents you can rent any of my easy parking vehicles for half price.

The Excuse Encyclopedia

14. THE PIZZA QUESTION

Would someone please explain to me why takeaway pizza comes in a square box?!?...

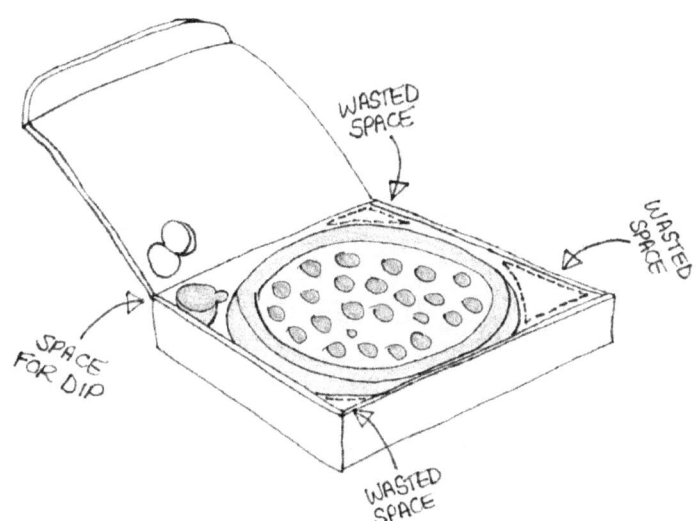

Book 4: Annoying Questions

15. THE SPACE QUESTION

If I was able to persuade the worlds space agencies to join together...

INTERNATIONAL
DEPARTMENT for the
INTERGALACTIC
OBSERVATIONS of
TIME and
SPACE

...could I call them I.D.I.O.T.S.

16. THE NATIONALITY QUESTION

If people who are born in America are called Americans, and people who born in Britain are called British...

... are people who are born in Malta called Malteasers?

17. THE GREAT FLOOD QUESTION

Were you friends with Noah or did you somehow survive the Great Flood? . . .

INVENTED BY MR WILLIAMS TO KEEP SINNERS AFLOAT.

. . . can we, your class of up-and-coming masterminds, trust you to set our homework when the alphabet poster in your classroom is clearly wrong!

The Excuse Encyclopedia

18. THE TOOTH QUESTION

What does the Tooth Fairy do with all the teeth she collects? . . .

. . . I have a couple of working theories but would welcome the input of an adult.

Book 4: Annoying Questions

19. THE CATERPILLAR QUESTION

Do butterflies remember life as a caterpillar?...

The Excuse Encyclopedia

20. THE CAR QUESTION

Instead of the classic car question - *'are we there yet?'* - try using SatNav lingo instead . . .

Book 4: Annoying Questions

21. THE SPELLING QUESTION

Why do some words have a silent 'K'? . . .

. . . knock, knickers, knapsack, knob, know, knee, knowledge, knuckles . . . There is no need! If you don't give me a valid reason by the weekend I will write an angry letter to the guy who wrote the dictionary.

22. THE EVOLUTION QUESTION

If man evolved from monkeys, then how come there are still loads of monkeys? ...

... are they the slow learners? The ones that didn't pass the evolution exam? Maybe they just prefer eating bananas to solving algebra?

23. THE ARK QUESTION

You know how in the Bible a man called Noah collected two of every animal, packed them on a huge boat and survived the Great Flood lasting forty days and forty nights . . .

. . . what did he do with the two woodpeckers? The only plausible explanation I can think of is that Noah invented the cork stopper.

24. THE RULE QUESTION

You know how there is an exception to every rule...

... is there an exception to that rule? Which would then mean that there is an exception to every rule apart from this one because the exception to this rule is that there is no exception negating the original exception... confused? Yeah, me too.

Book 4: Annoying Questions

25. THE CHOCOLATE QUESTION

Why is chocolate not considered to be a vegetable? . . .

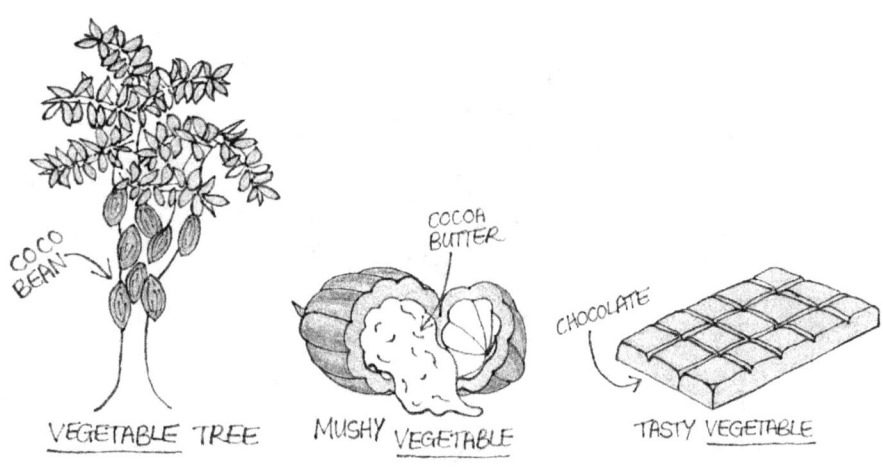

. . . chocolate is made from cocoa butter . . . which is found inside cocoa beans . . . which originate from the bean family . . . which is a vegetable. Therefore chocolate should be a vegetable.

26. THE SCIENCE QUESTION

Please explain how the Hydron Collider discovered the Higgs Boson Particle."* **

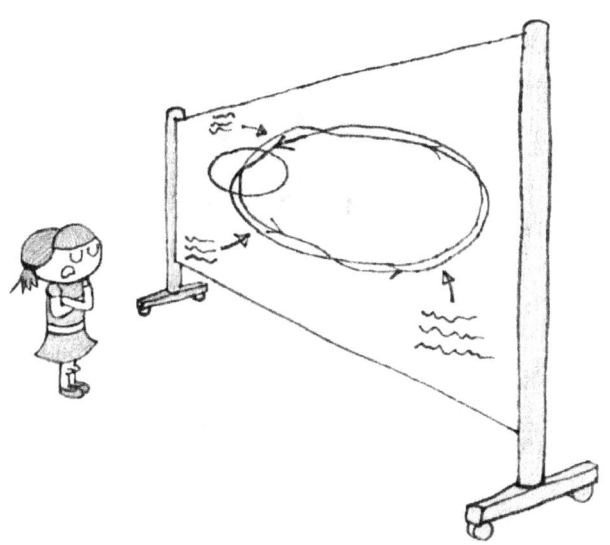

* ask this question then sit back and watch your parent let out a nervous giggle, turn red in the face, then flee to the nearest broom cupboard.

** this will only work if your parent is not called Dr Higgs Boson.

27. THE CHICKEN & EGG QUESTION

Which came first, the chicken or the egg?

. . . or perhaps some kind of chicken & egg mutant.

28. THE MEANING OF LIFE QUESTION

Why is the meaning of life so hard to discover?...

... I've got a dictionary, encyclopedia, Stephen Hawking on speed dial and a supercomputer but for some reason the only answer I ever get is the number 42!?

29. THE GAMES CONSOLE QUESTION

If God climbed down from his cloud and walked among us . . .

. . . would he buy a Playstation or an Xbox?

The Excuse Encyclopedia

30. THE BEES QUESTION

Do bees have knees? . . .

. . . also, do badgers carry daggers and do weasels drink diesel?

31. THE WAVE QUESTION

Who invented waving? . . .

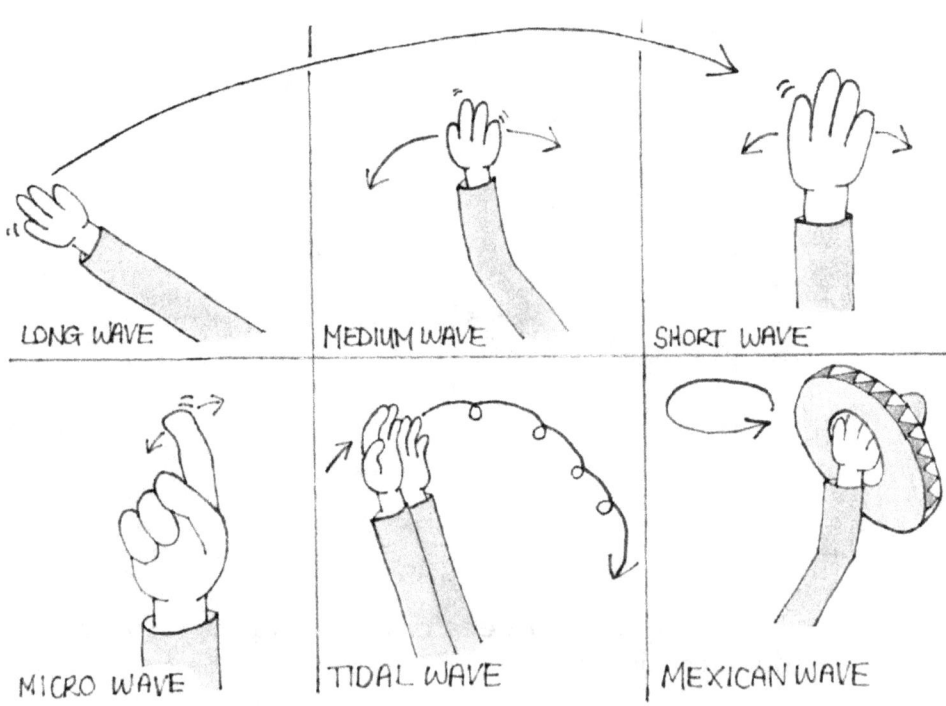

. . . once you find their contact details please let me know as I've got some fresh ideas they'd be interested in.

The Excuse Encyclopedia

32. THE NIPPLES QUESTION

Why . . . oh why . . .

. . . do men have nipples?

Book 4: Annoying Questions

33. THE PHILOSOPHICAL QUESTION

The classic philosophical question - *if a tree falls in a forest and no one is around to hear it, does it make a sound?* - that's so last century. So I've modernized it...

. . . if someone takes a selfie and shares it on Facebook but no one checks their timeline, does that person exist outside of our reality?

The Excuse Encyclopedia

34. THE COUNSELLING QUESTION

Counselling for addicts is a great idea...

... but what if the person becomes addicted to counselling?

Book 4: Annoying Questions

35. THE SCREEN QUESTION

If staring at a screen for too long will turn your eyes square, does it work for other objects as well? . . .

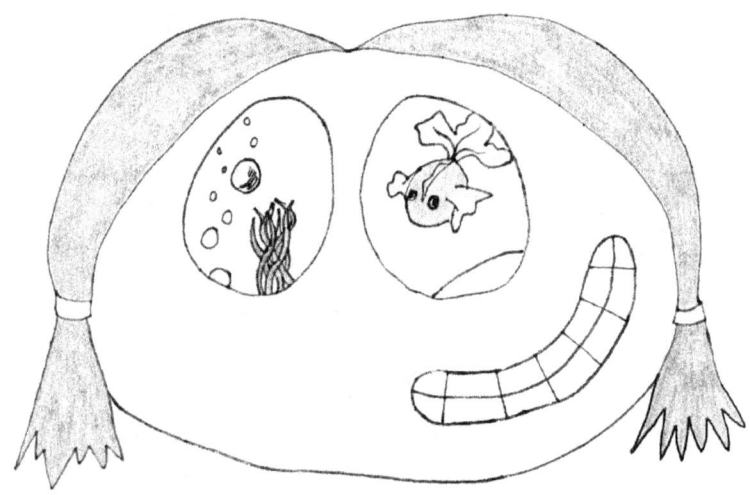

. . . if so, I am going to start staring at the fish bowl so that my pupils become little goldfish swimming around my eyeballs.

The Excuse Encyclopedia

36. THE WANDERING 'W' QUESTION

Why is there no 'w' in the word 'one', but there is a silent 'w' in the word 'two'? . . .

. . . somebody needs to help that 'w' find its way home.

Book 4: Annoying Questions

37. THE BUTTER QUESTION

Why does a piece of buttered toast always land butter side down? . . .

. . . I think it's time we found out whether butter is the culprit once and for all!

38. THE HEAVEN QUESTION

Once you have gone to heaven, are you stuck wearing the same clothes for all eternity?
...

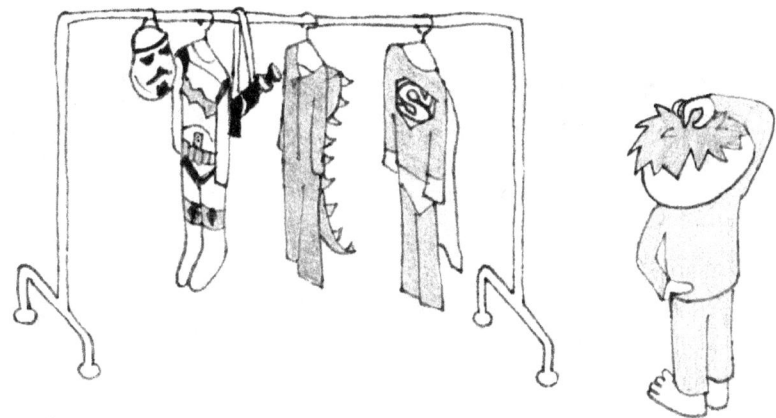

...if so I'm only wearing my best superhero costumes to bed from now on, just in case.

Book 4: Annoying Questions

39. THE TATTOO QUESTION

Our family trip to the beach has got me thinking...

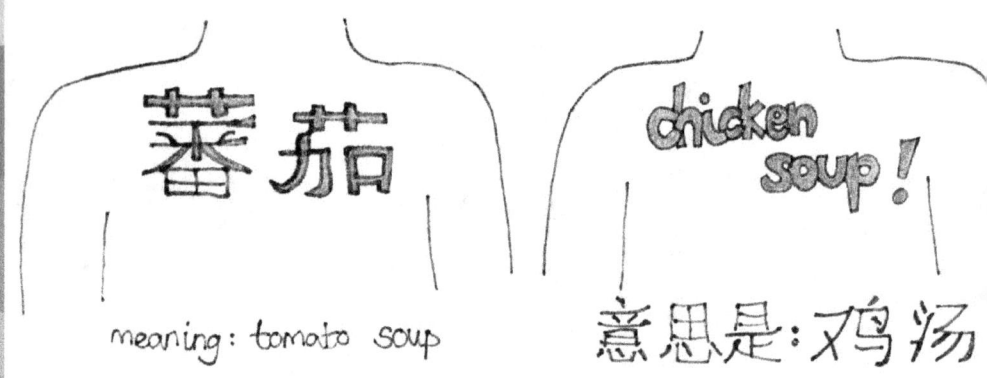

... do Chinese people get English words tattooed on their bodies?

40. THE ATHEIST QUESTION

You know how Atheists do not believe in a God . . .

. . . do you think that God does not believe in them either?

41. THE SPEED OF SMELL QUESTION

So we know the speed of light and we know the speed of sound . . .

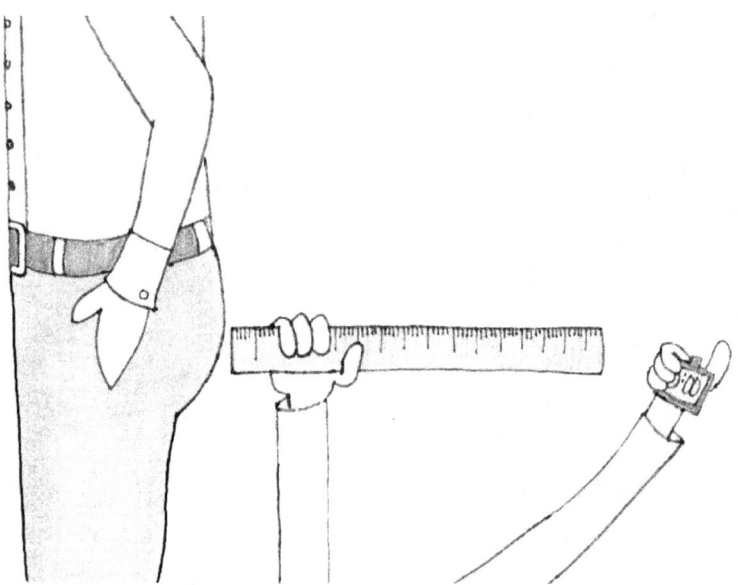

. . . but has anyone bothered to discover the speed of smell? Also could I borrow a peg please?

42. THE JOGGING QUESTION

I've been thinking, if exercise is so good for you then why do you never see a jogger smiling? . . .

. . . the people who eat chocolate, now they're the ones who look the happiest!

Book 4: Annoying Questions

43. THE CRUMPET QUESTION

How do crumpets get their little holes? .
. .

. . . I have some theories of my own I'd like to run them by an adult.

44. THE MARRIAGE QUESTION

You know Uncle Jim and Auntie Becca, how they say they've been together forever . . .

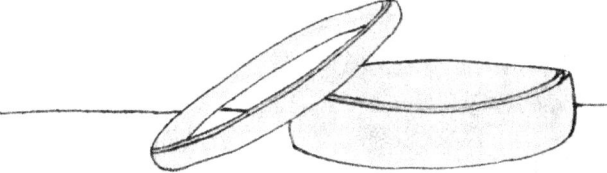

. . . does that mean that married people live longer than single people, or does it just seem longer?

Book 4: Annoying Questions

45. THE PYJAMA QUESTION

If dressing gowns and pyjamas are so comfy why does everyone get dressed into boring clothes every single morning? . . .

. . . we should boycott smart shirts and long skirts and beige trousers. Join the Pyjama Revolution and never be uncomfortable ever again!

46. THE ONION QUESTION

Why is it that every time you chop an onion you cry uncontrollably? ...

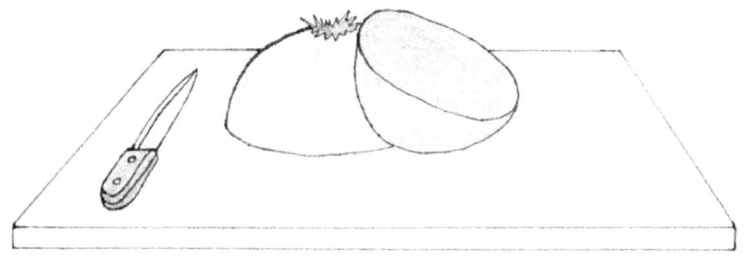

... did you have a traumatic childhood experience involving root vegetables? Did an onion try to kill you? There, there, I am here now, I won't let the mean onion hurt you.

Book 4: Annoying Questions

47. THE CANNIBAL QUESTION

Is it true that cannibals don't eat the following people:

CLOWNS	CATHOLIC MONKS
	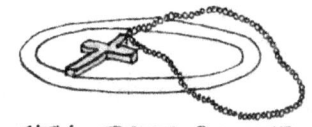
...THEY TASTE FUNNY	...THEY TASTE BETTER FRIAR-ED
THE HOMELESS	HAND MODELS
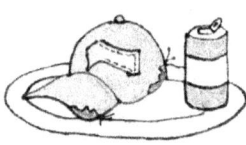	
...FREE RANGE TASTES HORRIBLE!!!	...ACTUALLY, THEY ARE FINGER-LICKING GOOD

The Excuse Encyclopedia

48. THE TONGUE-TWISTER QUESTION

If Peter Piper *really* did pick a pair of pickled peppers then . . .

. . . that would make him a lying, cheating thief! Peppers don't grow in pairs. The tongue twister should be *'Sneaky Steve stole a single salted sultana'.*

Book 4: Annoying Questions

49. THE HYPOTHETICAL QUESTION

Have you ever imagined a world without hypothetical situations? . . .

. . . nope, me neither.

The Excuse Encyclopedia

BONUS: AMERICAN FOOTBALL QUESTION

Dear Americans . . .

. . . Why do you call it 'football' when you use your hands instead of your feet (I think)?

BONUS: DICTIONARY QUESTION

Hello, I have a question...

... Is the word 'dictionary' in the dictionary?

The Excuse Encyclopedia

BONUS: FEATHER QUESTION

Humans find feathers extremely ticklish.

... Do birds find feathers ticklish too?

Book 4: Annoying Questions

BONUS: SLICED BREAD QUESTION

So . . .

Iced Bread

Diced Bread

Spliced Bread

. . . what was the best thing *before* sliced bread?

The Excuse Encyclopedia

BONUS: NATURAL BEAUTY QUESTION

Does spending three hours getting ready in the morning . . .

. . . help bring out your natural beauty?

Book 4: Annoying Questions

BONUS: NEW LIFE PHILOSOPHY QUESTION

Can I adopt this modern day life philosophy?...

...'if at first you don't succeed, complain about it on social media'.

BONUS: LOTTERY TICKET QUESTION

There, there, don't cry . . .

. . . my mother says that there are plenty of other people who don't win the lottery the first one thousand times too.

Book 4: Annoying Questions

BONUS: STRANGE ADULT QUESTION

Wow! You are surprisingly polite and well-educated for an adult . . .

. . . Are you the exception to the rule or some kind of freak science fair accident?

BONUS: CATS QUESTION

Don't cry...

× 23

... one day you're going to make one (or twenty-three) cats very happy.

BONUS: BEAR ARMS QUESTION

Why do Americans care so much about the right to bear arms? . . .

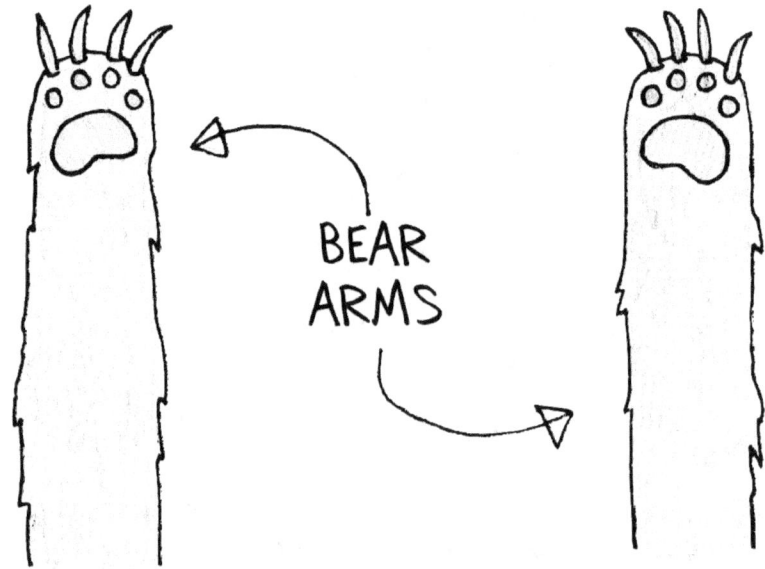

. . . (please spare a thought for all those poor armless American bears).

The Excuse Encyclopedia

BONUS: EMBARRASSING STORY QUESTION

What was your most embarrassing moment? . . .

. . . Please, just ignore all the recording devices. And I promise to never use this as blackmail.

Book 4: Annoying Questions

BONUS: MATHS QUESTION

Why do kids have to learn how to do maths in school...

SMARTPHONE (but also a calculator)

...when every single adult on the planet, if asked to do simple maths, just uses the calculator on their smartphone?

BOOK FIVE

Excuses for Skipping Gym Class

Book 5: Gym Class Excuses

1. THE DOCTORS NOTE EXCUSE

I've got a Doctor's Note for today lesson . . .

. . . turns out that sucking at sport is a newly discovered and extremely rare condition called *'Pretenditous'*. Unfortunately there is no known cure and as long as I have an active imagination I can't do Gym Class until I finish High School.

The Excuse Encyclopedia

2. THE LEARN-BY-EXAMPLE EXCUSE

As a keen and dedicated gym student...

...I feel I need a detailed demonstration of how to use every single piece of equipment in the school Gym. You can start with this one. I designed it myself.

Book 5: Gym Class Excuses

3. THE BULKING-UP EXCUSE

Sorry Coach, but I am currently in the middle of a bulk-up session...

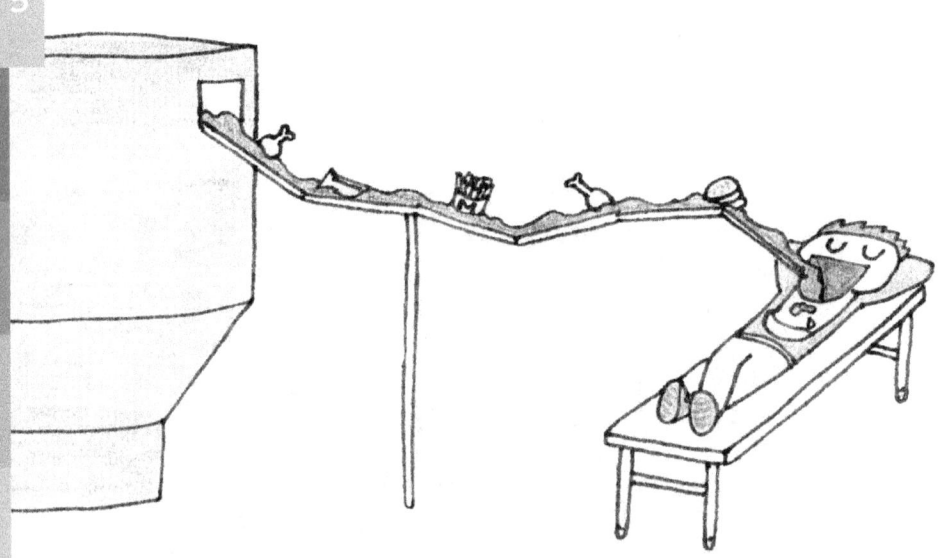

... as you can see this is an intense workout. Unfortunately I can not join in with the lesson until I have finished all this food, then slept for an hour, then completed another session I like to call *'the burp-a-thon'*.

The Excuse Encyclopedia

4. THE SUBSTITUTE EXCUSE

To learn the values of sportsmanship I have brought along my own substitute . . .

. . . she is really good at running and catching so, if I were you Coach, I would play her outfield.

Book 5: Gym Class Excuses

5. THE DEAD BALL EXCUSE

I have some terrible news, Coach. Spalding is dead...

... when we returned him to the cupboard yesterday he was fine. This morning we opened the door and found him like this. The whole class are devastated by this awful tragedy. See you in 6 months.

6. THE ROBOTS EXCUSE

Modern technology is moving closer and closer towards artificial intelligence and this school has also encouraged the pursuit of progress and achievement. So . . .

. . . here are my robots. The first one tells everyone what to do, the second crushes anyone who disobeys and the last one cleans up the mess. They will take over from here so I can do more important stuff.

7. THE SLEEP WALKING EXCUSE

I have already had my daily recommended amount of exercise . . .

. . . last night to be exact.

The Excuse Encyclopedia

8. THE FITNESS PROGRAMME EXCUSE

Thanks to my new fitness programme I don't need to do Gym Class ever again . . .

. . . I simply turn my head to the left, then turn my head to the right, then back to the left again. I do this every time someone offers me a cookie.

Book 5: Gym Class Excuses

9. THE MUSCULAR EXCUSE

I'm afraid I can not take part in Gym Class anymore...

...my muscles are completely full! If I lifted another weight my arms will explode.

10. THE SOCKS EXCUSE

My socks, they . . . they don't . . . they don't match . . .

. . . the ancient prophecy has come true. Run for your lives, save yourselves . . . THE APOCALYPSE IS COMING!

Book 5: Gym Class Excuses

11. THE PRAYER EXCUSE

I'm trading in Gym Class for prayer...

Dear Lord,
If you can not make me skinny then please make the rest of my class rounder...
Amen.

...if this works it'll benefit everyone. You can thank me later.

12. THE NATURE EXCUSE

Look at these examples from nature...

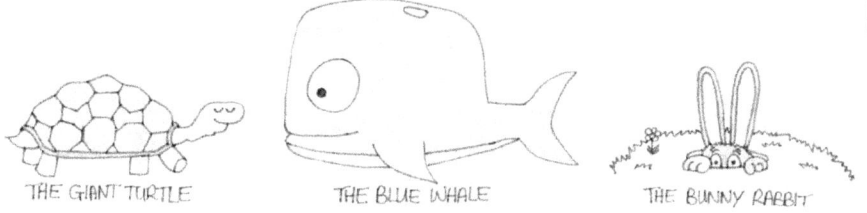

THE GIANT TURTLE   THE BLUE WHALE   THE BUNNY RABBIT

...the Giant Turtle: sleeps for 16 hours a day and has a lifespan of 100 years. The Blue Whale: eats 4 tons of krill a day and has a lifespan of 80 years. The Bunny Rabbit: eats mainly grass or hay, can reach speeds of 18 miles an hour and has a lifespan of 3 years. It seems nature is telling me to eat, sleep and not exercise to live a long and happy life.

13. THE FLOWER EXCUSE

I have decided to trade in my legs for a stem . . .

. . . I'm now a flower that can only be watered with Lucozade. If you need me I will be in the planet pot next to the 52" Flat Screen TV in the Teachers Lounge.

14. THE ACCIDENT EXCUSE

I've had a terrible accident Coach . . .

. . . I was practicing doing a forward roll when it happened. Looks like I will have to spend the rest of my life as a ball.

15. THE R.S.P.C.S. EXCUSE

I have started a new school society called the R.S.P.C.S. . . .

. . . it is our responsibility to protect and care for sport in its natural habitat. For far too long this school has exploited and enslaved sport by means of enforced labour and cruelty. It stops now. We say NO to sports slavery. Join my society and boycott Gym Class before endangered sports become extinct.

The Excuse Encyclopedia

16. THE LOST PROPERTY EXCUSE

Listen, how about we make a deal . . .

. . . if you cancel Gym Class you can have anything from the lost property box and none of us will tell on you. And if you let us play on our phones I'll write a letter to the Headteacher explaining how I think you deserve a massive pay rise and a company sports car.

Book 5: Gym Class Excuses

17. THE LETTER EXCUSE

I have a letter from my parents...

...it explains why I can not do Gym Class today. And if that doesn't work I have also got letters from the Queen of England and Arnold Schwarzenegger.

The Excuse Encyclopedia

18. THE CONSPIRACY EXCUSE

Don't overreact, but I think the new Gym Teachers are killing off the weedy kids...

... why do I think they're murderers? How else can you explain the fact that there's only ever muscular kids at the Gym these days?

19. THE CHEWING EXCUSE

I realised something last night, I am really good at one exercise . . .

. . . chewing! Earlier in the year you told us - *'practice makes perfect'* - so I'll be over here training really really hard.

The Excuse Encyclopedia

20. THE VIDEO GAMER EXCUSE

Unfortunately I can't join in today . . .

. . . if I do 10 laps of the pitch then I won't have any energy left to play video games tonight. Sorry but I have got priorities to consider.

Book 5: Gym Class Excuses

21. THE DEATH STAR EXCUSE

Good news Coach. I've been accepted into the *'Death Star Internship Programme'*...

... it was nice training with you all but becoming an Intergalactic Overlord in a giant circular spaceship is my destiny. Plus I've already checked and there is no Gym Class at Sith School.

22. THE NEW EXERCISES EXCUSE

I have developed some new exercises for the class to try...

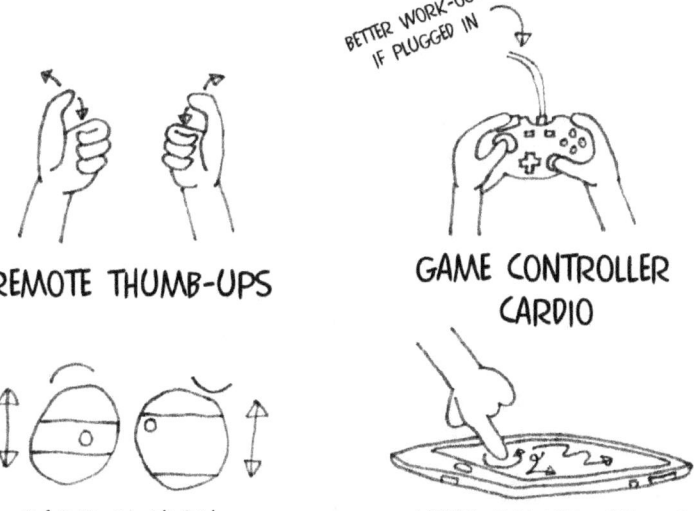

REMOTE THUMB-UPS

BETTER WORK-OUT IF PLUGGED IN

GAME CONTROLLER CARDIO

RAPID BLINKING

INDEX FINGER CURLS

...the great thing about my revolutionary exercises is that you do all of them sitting down. In fact you don't even have to change into your gym kit. Amazing, I know.

Book 5: Gym Class Excuses

23. THE PHONE CALL EXCUSE

I just got the most important phone call of my entire life . . .

. . . the President of the United States of America is on his way. Quickly, get into a line and salute while standing completely motionless like they do on TV. Otherwise the President might take offence and throw us all in jail.

The Excuse Encyclopedia

24. THE FORTUNE TELLER EXCUSE

I was going to do Gym Class today...

...but my Fortune Teller advised me to stay away from all forms of exercise. Something about a *'foreboding accident'*, sounds painful doesn't it.

25. THE TOOTH EXCUSE

According to my dentist this tooth is dangerously close to falling out . . .

. . . and according to the Tooth Fairy if I lose a tooth while doing a roly-poly my tooth is void of all monetary value. Everyone knows she does not except any teeth that have travelled through the body's digestive system!

The Excuse Encyclopedia

26. THE JIM EXCUSE

So it turns out I've been going to the Gym for months and months . . .

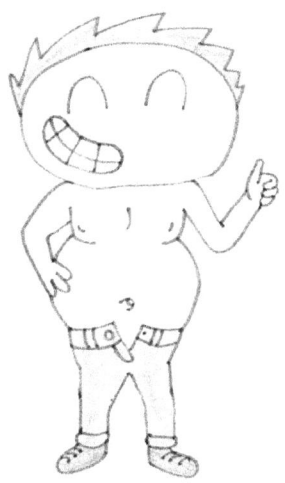

. . . the guy who always serves me at McDonalds is called Jim! I know, great isn't it. Maybe we should take the whole class to Jim now and have a workout at the fastfood joint.

Book 5: Gym Class Excuses

27. THE HAND-STAND EXCUSE

Good news, I have mastered the handstand . . .

. . . took me all night to construct this masterpiece but just take a look at the beauty. Look how it balances my hand perfectly while I am in a standing position. It's so good I made one for my foot too.

28. THE PROTEIN SUPPLEMENT EXCUSE

This just arrived for me . . .

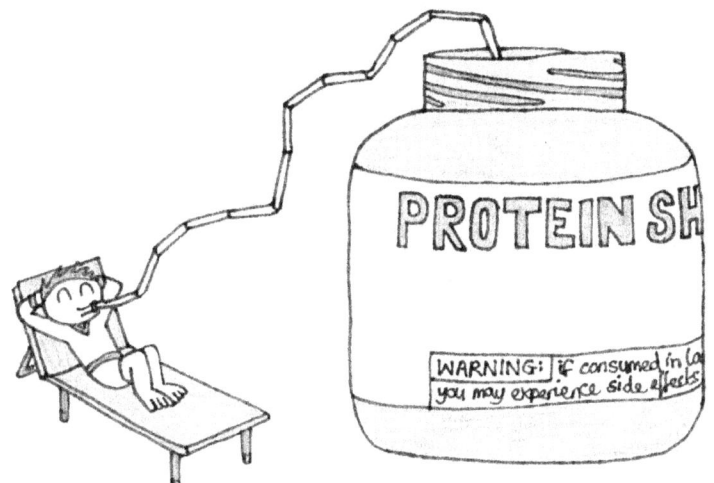

. . . so I don't need to do Gym Class today, I'll drink this instead.

Book 5: Gym Class Excuses

29. THE BRIEFCASE EXCUSE

Oh dear. This isn't my gym kit...

... I must have picked up the wrong bag, but if anyone is interested I could do my Dad's presentation on the quarterly stats.

The Excuse Encyclopedia

30. THE CHESTNUT EXCUSE

The new chestnut diet I have been trialling for Heat Magazine has been causing two very annoying problems . . .

. . . number 1. I smell like a giant chestnut, and number 2. this gang of squirrels keeps on trying to kidnap me and bury me underneath a tree for the winter months.

31. THE NEW SPORT EXCUSE

I have invented a new sport. I call it *'Xtreme Simon Says'*...

...it is exactly the same as normal *'Simon Says'* except it is just for Teachers and if you get it wrong Gretel from the senior Dodgeball Team will throw this ball at you. Ready, steady, GO!

32. THE EVIL PLOT EXCUSE

My plot to overthrow the school council is almost complete . . .

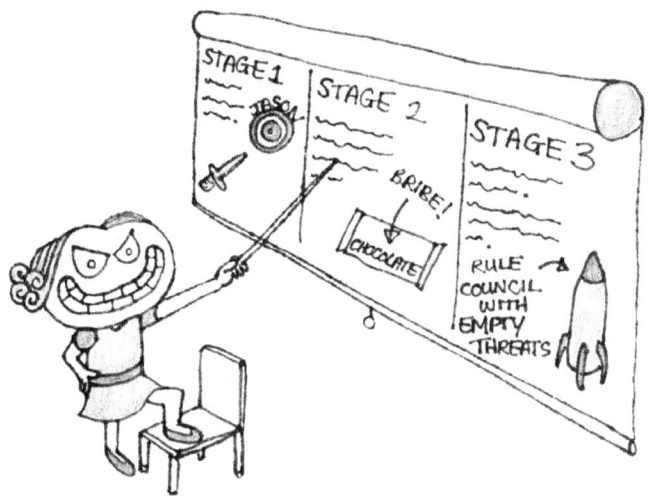

. . . I'm thinking of changing things up, you know, move away from democracy and try a dictatorship. So if you give me some time to finalise my plans I'll make you number 2. How does that sound?

Book 5: Gym Class Excuses

33. THE ANTI-SPORT EXCUSE

Coach, I think there is something wrong with me . . .

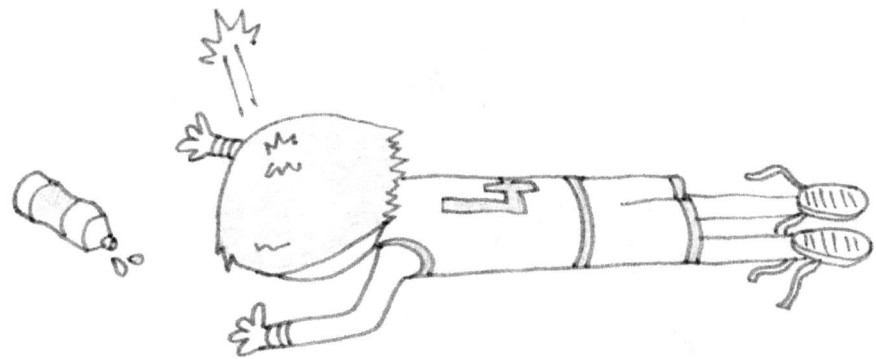

. . . when I exercise my cheeks turn red, my armpits smell, my breathing doubles and my heartbeat triples. Surely the only possible explanation is that I am allergic to exercise.

34. THE FRIES EXCUSE

Pardon Coach, today in Gym Class we are going to *'do some exercise'* . . .

. . . I thought you said *'bring extra-fries'*. I spent a months worth of pocket money on all these fries and it is too late to take them back now. We can not let them go to waste now, can we?

Book 5: Gym Class Excuses

35. THE POKEMON EXCUSE

I think I misunderstood what today's lesson is about...

...I thought you said *'we will be training up to battle the Gym Leader'*, instead of *'we will be training up on the gym equipment'*.

The Excuse Encyclopedia

36. THE EMPTY BELLY EXCUSE

As you can see there is no food in my belly . . .

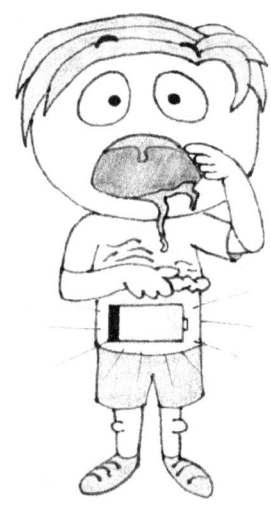

. . . I'm running dangerously low on power. How can you expect me, a growing lad, to do strenuous exercise without the proper energy source required?

Book 5: Gym Class Excuses

37. THE TORNADO EXCUSE

Holy Moley! Tornado Doris just passed through the Gym Cupboard . . .

. . . don't go in there Coach, don't even poke your head in. The destruction to the gym equipment will be extremely upsetting to someone of your profession. I recommend that we all head to the local checkpoint, declare ourselves alive and take some time to mourn our destroyed-beyond-repair school equipment.

38. THE BRAIN EXCUSE

I understand that my body needs exercise . . .

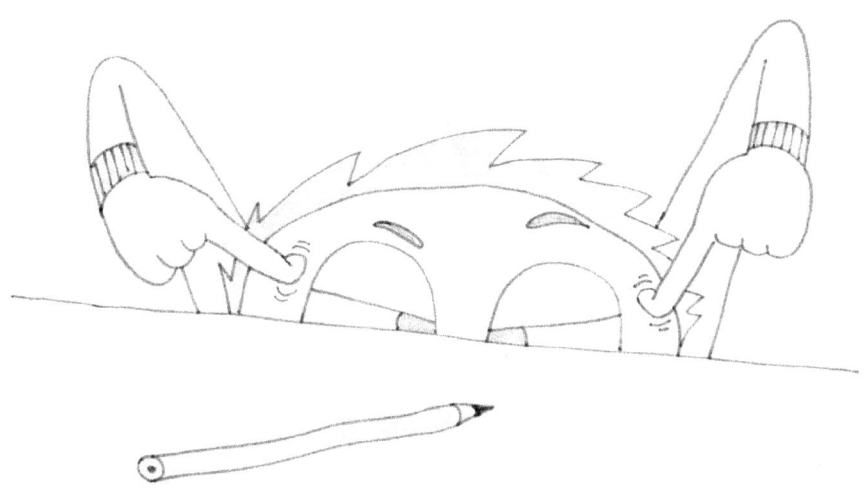

. . . but so does my brain, right? With this in mind I'll be doing some brain training instead of running laps today. If you need me I will be in the corner attempting to move this pencil with my mind.

Book 5: Gym Class Excuses

39. THE DIGESTION EXCUSE

Sorry but I cannot do any strenuous exercise for the next two hours . . .

. . . I ate a large portion of chips for lunch and polished off the emergency chocolate bars you keep in the bottom draw in your office. Two hours is the recommended amount of nap-time required for healthy digestion so please try to keep the noise down Coach.

40. THE EXPERIMENT EXCUSE

We have been learning about the extraordinary metabolism of adult Gym Teachers in Science Class. So . . .

. . . I was wondering if you would run on this treadmill for two hours while I monitor your metabolism levels for my homework.

Book 5: Gym Class Excuses

41. THE ONE RING EXCUSE

I was practising long jump when I landed on this ring . . .

. . . there's some funny-looking writing around the edge. So I guess that means I've got to go on a really really long journey and toss it in a volcano. Wish me luck!

The Excuse Encyclopedia

42. THE RAIN DANCE EXCUSE

I found this costume in the cupboard Coach...

... then all of a sudden my ancestral instincts took over and I began dancing and chanting and jumping like a frog around this fire until it started to rain. Guess that means we can't do outdoor games, darn you unpredictable weather.

43. THE DEMON GYM TEACHER EXCUSE

I am the Demon Gym Teacher and I am here for Miss Jones . . .

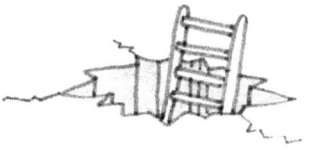

. . . you have been summoned to stand trial for crimes against students. I recommend finding yourself a good lawyer as the jury down in Hell will be a tough crowd, they all hated Gym Class too.

The Excuse Encyclopedia

44. THE PHOTO-BOMBER EXCUSE

Good news everyone. I've got a job as a professional Photo-Bomber...

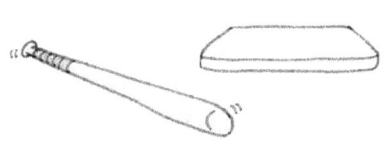

... I am on call 24/7. Oh, just got a call. A happy couple is about to take a selfie one mile east from here. See you later everyone, got a photo to ruin.

Book 5: Gym Class Excuses

45. THE PAPER CUT EXCUSE

I've been looking forward to Gym Class all week but . . .

. . . unfortunately it happened again. Look, I've got a debilitating paper cut. It's 6mm deep and 8mm long this time. I think Art Class doesn't want me to exercise because this seems to happen every week.

46. THE FORGETFUL EXCUSE

Sorry Coach, I have forgotten my gym clothes...

... I must be having a forgetful day because I have also forgotten who poured petrol over the spare clothes box and set it on fire.

Book 5: Gym Class Excuses

47. THE SCHOOL TOILET EXCUSE

The new school toilets just tried to kill me . . .

. . . the flush almost drowned me, the soap dispenser blinded me and the hand dryer made my hair look like this. I think I need to sit down for the next hour or so to recover.

48. THE ALLERGIES EXCUSE

Bad news Coach, I'm allergic to sport balls . . .

. . . so unless we all play with this imaginary basketball my doctor has given me I can not join in with today's lesson.

49. THE NEW T-SHIRT EXCUSE

Look Coach, I've bought a new t-shirt . . .

. . . all I have to do now is wait. I decided to go for the XXXL size to allow for plenty of space once the loading process is complete.

BONUS: DREAMS EXCUSE

I know you want me to run around the school field, but . . .

. . . I'm going back to bed. Why? Because I'm following your excellent advise - to never, ever give up on my *dreams*.

Book 5: Gym Class Excuses

BONUS: HOGWARTS LETTER EXCUSE

I'm way too emotional to doing ANYTHING! . . .

. . . I have finally received a reply from Hogwarts. They have rejected my application.

BONUS: NEW WATCH EXCUSE

Great news, I've bought a brand new fitness watch...

...As the Gym Class teacher I know that your fitness watch must be telling you that you've got a chance. However, mine is telling me to just give up and go eat a brownie.

Book 5: Gym Class Excuses

BONUS: DOUGHNUTS EXCUSE

Sir, I'm struggling to lose weight . . .

. . . What's my fitness and diet plan? I go for a run to the bakery and then eat an entire tray of doughnuts.

BONUS: ICE-CREAM EXCUSE

I believe you can pass Gym Class* . . .

. . . *(by bribing the teacher with lots and lots of ice cream).

Book 5: Gym Class Excuses

BONUS: SWEATY EXCUSE

I can't run around the school field five times today...

...I've got a phobia for sweating. Sweat freaks me out! It's like smelly water that pours out from your armpits and dribbles all the way down to your socks. GROSS!!!

BONUS: JELLY LEGS EXCUSE

I would normally leap at the opportunely to run around the school field, but . . .

. . . I ran a 1,000,000k race yesterday. I won, of course. And now my legs have literally turned into jelly.

Book 5: Gym Class Excuses

BONUS: OUT OF CHARGE EXCUSE

Do you have a fitness watch? . . .

. . . So do I, and because I'm so fit it's always out of charge. So, I'll be ready to take part in today's Gym Class lesson in four to six hours.

BONUS: SLUG EXCUSE

I've created a new fitness training routine inspired by slugs . . .

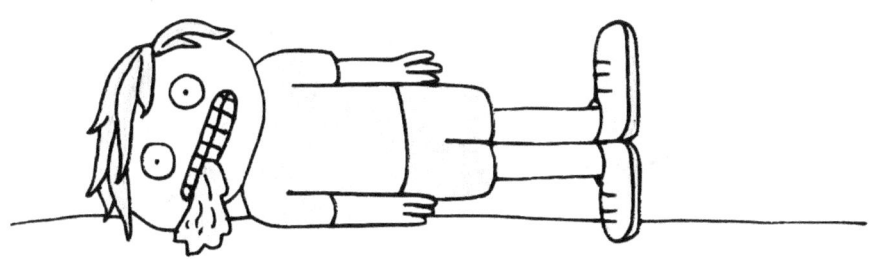

. . . Everyone and anyone can do it. It involves lying on the floor, eating lots of lettuce, more lying down and doing ABSOLUTELY nothing else.

Book 5: Gym Class Excuses

BONUS: EXAM EXCUSE

LOOK! I passed the Ultimate Gym Class Written Exam . . .

. . . I have nothing more to gain from Gym Class, so I won't be attending your lessons anymore and will be going to the School Library to 'study' instead.

BONUS: ARMPIT OF DOOM EXCUSE

Stand back! It's for your own safety...

... Why? Because my armpits smell like three-day-old baked beans. If I do Gym Class today, all the other students WILL pass out.

BONUS: ULTIMATE GYM EXAM EXCUSE

I'm taking the Ultimate Gym Class Exam . . .

. . . It's a written exam. So, instead of running around aimlessly in the freezing cold weather today I'll be sitting in this lovely and warm room for the next two hours.

BOOK SIX

Excuses for Staying Up Past Your Bedtime

Book 6: Bedtime Excuses

1. THE UNDER THE BED EXCUSE

Mum, I don't want to alarm you but there is something under my bed . . .

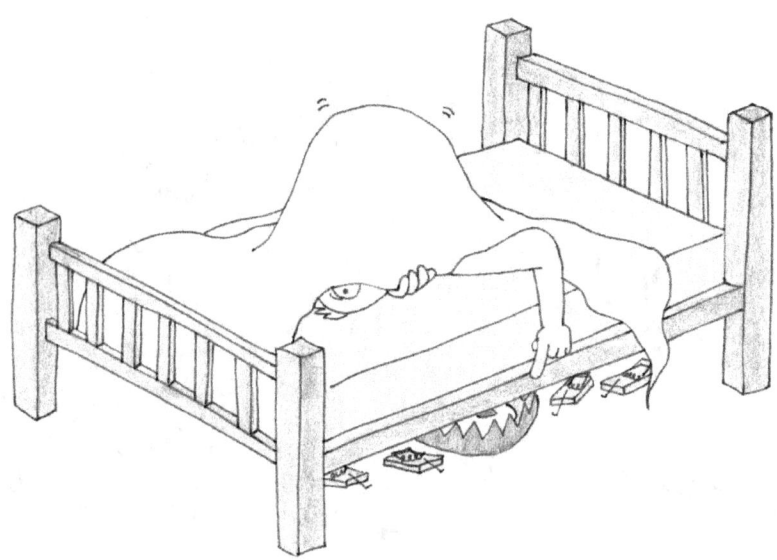

. . . You are not allowed to turn off the light until I am 100% sure there are no monsters hiding under there. Could you check it for me please?

2. THE EVIL TEDDY EXCUSE

I would go to bed, in fact I want to go to bed. It's just . . .

. . . My teddy bear is evil! Ever since we put him in the washing machine after I dropped him in that muddy puddle, Marshmallow has been looking at me funny. It's like he is waiting for me to fall asleep . . . *to exact his revenge.*

3. THE MORNING EXCUSE

What? Go to bed? But it's the morning...

... The sun has risen and the cockerel has crowed. I had a lovely sleep and I am ready to take on a new day. Can I have a bowl of cereal please?

The Excuse Encyclopedia

4. THE INSOMNIA EXCUSE

I've been reading medical journals and doing online research . . .

. . . I have Insomnia: a terrible sleeping disorder which means I can't fall asleep. Honestly, I've tried everything. I just can't fall asleep!

5. THE MEDICAL BREAKTHROUGH EXCUSE

At last my work is complete. Behold the 'Stay-Up-All-Night Pill'...

... *Gulp* What did you say? Don't swallow the pill. Too late, Dad. Now I've got to stay up all night and make a list of all the side-effects I experience. Is the room spinning or are my eyeballs rolling around on the floor?

The Excuse Encyclopedia

6. THE TEMPERATURE EXCUSE

I'M TOO HOT, I NEED TO TAKE MY VEST OFF

NOW I'M TOO COLD, I NEED TO PUT ON THICKER SOCKS

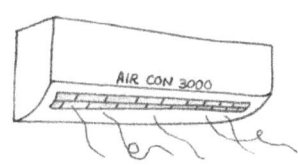

NOW I'M TOO HOT AGAIN, TURN THE AIR CON TO FULL POWER

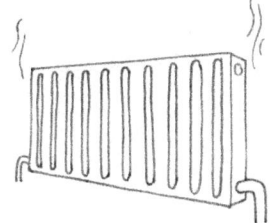

NOW I'M TOO COLD AGAIN, TURN THE RADIATOR TO FULL POWER

. . . Repeat until you've run out of ideas, then claim to be suffering from sunstroke and hypothermia at the same time.

Book 6: Bedtime Excuses

7. THE NIGHT SCHOOL TRIP EXCUSE

What does it look like I'm doing? I'm packing for the night school trip . . .

. . . Strange, I thought I told you about my class star gazing expedition. Anyway, I can't talk now, I've got lots of packing to do.

8. THE STUCK IN THE BATH EXCUSE

Thanks to my new fitness programme I don't need to do Gym Class ever again . . .

. . . I simply turn my head to the left, then turn my head to the right, then back to the left again. I do this every time someone offers me a cookie.

9. THE STORYTIME EXCUSE

I do miss the days when you'd read me a bedtime story . . .

. . . So I decided to glue together all my Harry Potter Books. Now you can read them to me back to back in one sitting. I'm ready when you are.

The Excuse Encyclopedia

10. THE MONDAYS EXCUSE

I can't go sleep. It's Sunday night...

...If we all go to bed then we are allowing Monday - the worst of all the days - to creep up and shackle us to another week. But not me, I'm going to live in between the weekend and the week forever and ever. Go on, try and stop me!

Book 6: Bedtime Excuses

11. THE RESTRAINING ORDER EXCUSE

Bad news, my bed has filed a restraining order against me . . .

. . . I can't go within 25 feet of my bed or I'll be thrown in jail. The bed lawyers told me that it felt unappreciated and was tired of being walked all over.

12. THE X-MEN EXCUSE

Finally, I've been accepted. Xaviers School for Gifted Children have recognised my genetic mutation . . .

. . . I don't sleep. My brain never needs to rest and my muscles regenerate all by themselves. So I can make the morning brew and do all the cleaning while all the other X-Men are fast asleep.

Book 6: Bedtime Excuses

13. THE HUNGRY SOFA EXCUSE

Help! The sofa is trying to eat me . . .

. . . I've probably got two hours left to live until the sofa has finished slowly digesting me. Goodbye Mum, goodbye Dad. My one dying wish is for you to switch the TV back on and bring me a glass of milk and a cookie.

14. THE WORK EXPERIENCE EXCUSE

Did you get the letter from school explaining my work experience programme starts tonight...

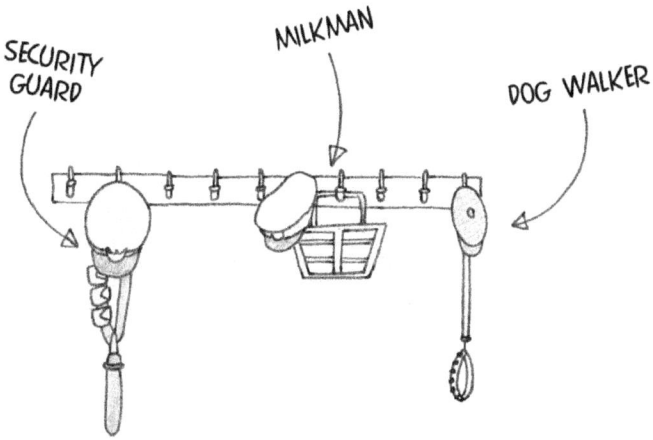

... From 8pm – 2am I'll be a Security Guard, from 2am – 6am I'll be a Milkman, and from 6am – 8am I'll be a Dog Walker. Wish me luck on my first night shift.

15. THE NEGOTIATION EXCUSE

I know that my bedtime is normally 8pm and my older brother goes to bed at 10pm, but . . .

. . . Me and my older brother have had a mature conversation and we've decided that it would be better for both of us if you were to swap our bedtimes.

16. THE GOLDEN MOON EXCUSE

I can't go to bed now, otherwise I'll miss a once-in-a-million years phenomenon . . .

. . . It's called *The Golden Moon*. What does it look like? Well let me stay up all night and we can find out together.

Book 6: Bedtime Excuses

17. THE SELF-TORTURE EXCUSE

I've forgotten where I left my homework . . .

. . . So now I've got to torture the information out of myself. If I were you I'd leave me to it. This could get ugly.

18. THE STUDYING EXCUSE

I have decided to take your advice and read more books...

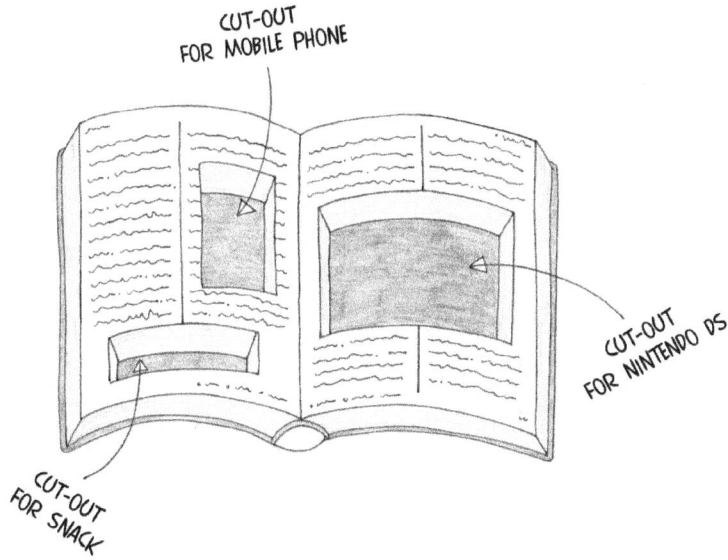

...why do I think they're murderers? How else can you explain the fact that there's only ever muscular kids at the Gym these days?

Book 6: Bedtime Excuses

19. THE LIST OF DEMANDS EXCUSE

Of course mama, I'll go to bed like a nice little girl . . .

. . . as soon as you have completed this list of demands!

The Excuse Encyclopedia

20. THE MISSING TEDDY EXCUSE

Oh no, Teddy is missing. I can't go to bed without Teddy . . .

. . . I must have left him at Grandma's house. I think Teddy is inside Grandma's unbreakable safe behind the secret door hidden at the bottom of the locked basement. I'll wait in my bedroom until you've found Teddy and brought him back.

21. THE CONCOCTION EXCUSE

There was once a boy called George who had a marvellous idea...

... He has inspired me to make my very own marvellous medicine to help me stay up all night. If you need me I'll be bouncing from one wall to the next until morning.

The Excuse Encyclopedia

22. THE SUPPER EXCUSE

I can't go to bed until I've had my supper . . .

. . . I'd like a three course supper tonight. I'll start with the French Onion Soup with Parmesan Croutons. For main I'll have the Pigeon Breast in Red Wine with Potatoes Au Gratin. And for dessert the Vanilla Crème Brûlée with Goji Berries . . . And don't forget the Tomato Ketchup.

Book 6: Bedtime Excuses

23. THE SELF-HYPNOTISM EXCUSE

I bought this self-hypnotism kit from the internet to help with my bedtime . . .

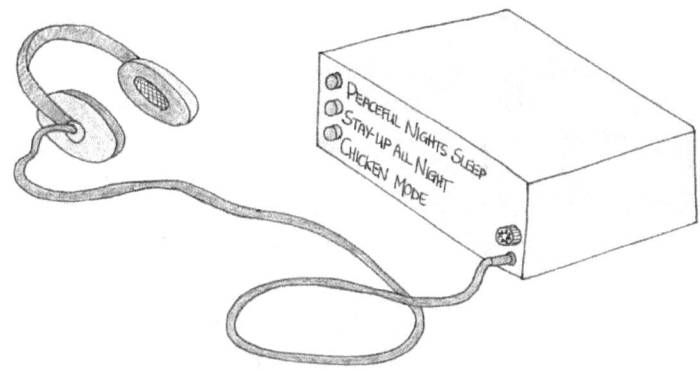

. . . The only problem is that the User Manual is missing. It looks very confusing. I do hope I get this right.

24. THE BRAIN FLU EXCUSE

I can't fall asleep. I think I have Brain Flu . . .

. . . What? You haven't heard of Brain Flu? It is a terrible disease of the brain that can turn you into a vegetable and the only cure is to starve your brain of sleep by staying up all night. Oh yeah, and it is highly contagious and transmitted through brain waves.

Book 6: Bedtime Excuses

25. THE PRACTISING EXCUSE

Pardon, did you ask me what I am doing?

. . .

. . . I am practising to become a professional ballet dancer, a world-class musician and a plate spinning champion all at the same time. I can't waste my precious time on *sleep*. Trust me, when I'm winning awards and making millions I'll remember how you let me stay up all night to practise and mention you in my acceptance speeches.

26. THE THIRSTY EXCUSE

I'm really thirsty, can I have a drink please? . . .

. . . Oh dear, now I really need a wee, can I go to the toilet? Now I'm thirsty again, can I have a drink please? Now I need a wee again . . . *repeat until your parent looks angry, then suggest they should drink a glass of water to calm down.*

27. THE WET THE BED EXCUSE

Mum, I've got something embarrassing to tell you . . .

. . . I mistook my bedroom for the bathroom and wet the bed. I thought the taps were some sort of new feature to control the heated mattress. Please don't tell any of my friends about this.

The Excuse Encyclopedia

28. THE WINSTON CHURCHILL EXCUSE

Did you know that Winston Churchill only had 3 hours of sleep a night while he was planning the D-Day landings . . .

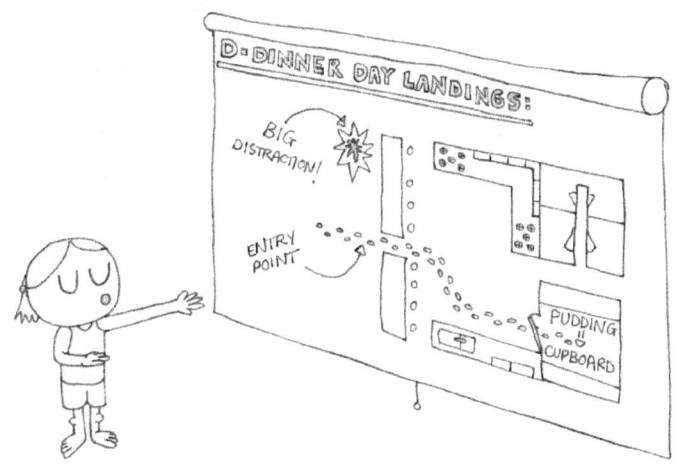

. . . I'm planning something similar. I'm planning the D-D-Day Landings. I am going to infiltrate enemy territory in a covert operation to steal highly classified school secrets. So I will need to stay up all night for the rest of the week to perfect my plans.

Book 6: Bedtime Excuses

29. THE CRICKETS EXCUSE

The crickets outside are very loud, aren't they . . .

. . . What are they saying? Why do they talk so loud? When do they go to sleep? How do the birds sleep while the crickets are talking? Where do birds sleep? When do they wake up?

The Excuse Encyclopedia

30. THE TOOTH TRAP EXCUSE

What, go to bed? But I need to stay up all night and hold this rope . . .

. . . I am going to do what no child has done before. I am going to catch the Tooth Fairy.

Book 6: Bedtime Excuses

31. THE PHONE CALL EXCUSE

Is that the phone, don't worry I'll get it . . .

. . . Hello this is Jimmy speaking *pause* what, you've captured Scooby Doo, Ash Ketchum and SpongeBob Square Pants *pause* they are dangling over a tank of sharks with laser beams attached their tails *pause* and you're going to cut the rope if I stop playing videos games all night *pause* ok, ok, I'll play video games all night, just don't kill my favourite TV characters!

The Excuse Encyclopedia

32. THE CHINA EXCUSE

I know it is 9pm, so it's time for bed . . .

. . . but I've decided I'm Chinese now. It's 9am in China so I better go, I'm late for school.

33. THE BED BUGS EXCUSE

You know how you bought me that microscope for my birthday . . .

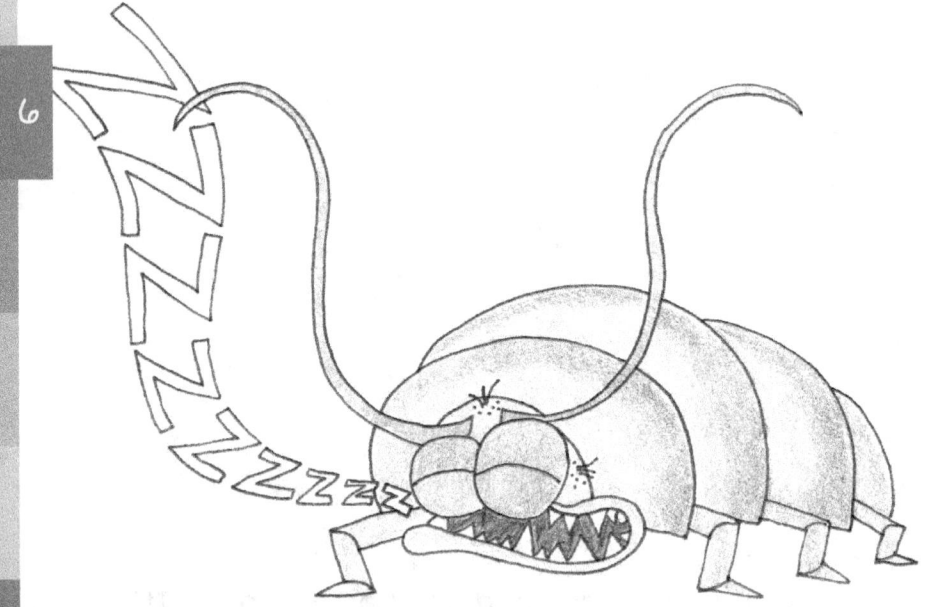

. . . I found this mutant Bed Bug in my pillow. I hope you agree I can't share a bed with that thing, it clearly snores and will probably steal the duvet!

34. THE COUNTING SHEEP EXCUSE

Tonight I'd like to try a new idea to help me fall asleep . . .

. . . Apparently counting sheep helps you sleep so I've built a fence and designed these sheep costumes. If you and Dad and Grandma and Grandpa and my older brother could wear them and jump over this fence I would be very grateful.

35. THE EYELIDS EXCUSE

I don't want to go to sleep . . .

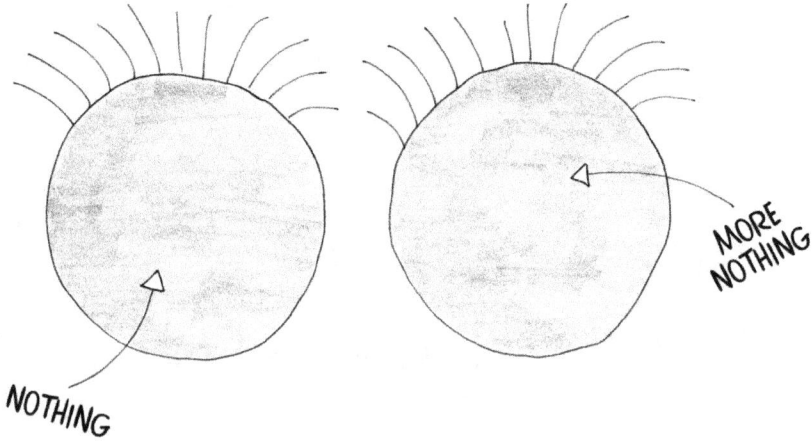

. . . The insides of my eyelids are soooooooooooooooooooooooooooooo boring to look at!

The Excuse Encyclopedia

36. THE UNCOMFORTABLE EXCUSE

I can't go to sleep. My bed is really uncomfortable . . .

. . . Don't panic, I've taken care of it. Would anyone like a marshmallow on a stick? Oh, and I need a new bed.

Book 6: Bedtime Excuses

37. THE KISS GOODNIGHT EXCUSE

I forgot to give you a goodnight kiss and while I am downstairs I might as well say goodnight to everyone I love...

GOODNIGHT KITCHEN CHAIR

GOODNIGHT TV

GOODNIGHT DOOR HANDLE

GOODNIGHT KNIVES, FORKS & SPOONS

GOODNIGHT BOOKS

GOODNIGHT CURTAINS

...here are some ideas for items you can kiss goodnight. Remember, the possibilities are endless, but I would recommend staying away from the toilet.

The Excuse Encyclopedia

38. THE SUNRISE EXCUSE

Science *thinks* it knows everything, but I've made a ground-breaking discovery! . . .

. . . The Sun does not rise every morning because the Earth is orbiting the Sun whilst spinning at 1,041mph. It will only rise if I stay up all night praying to the Moon Goddess so she releases her pet galactic space beetle which pushes the Sun over the horizon and across the sky.

Book 6: Bedtime Excuses

39. THE WHALE EXCUSE

I've been reading on the internet that Whale Song is a relaxing and soothing way to drop off to sleep . . .

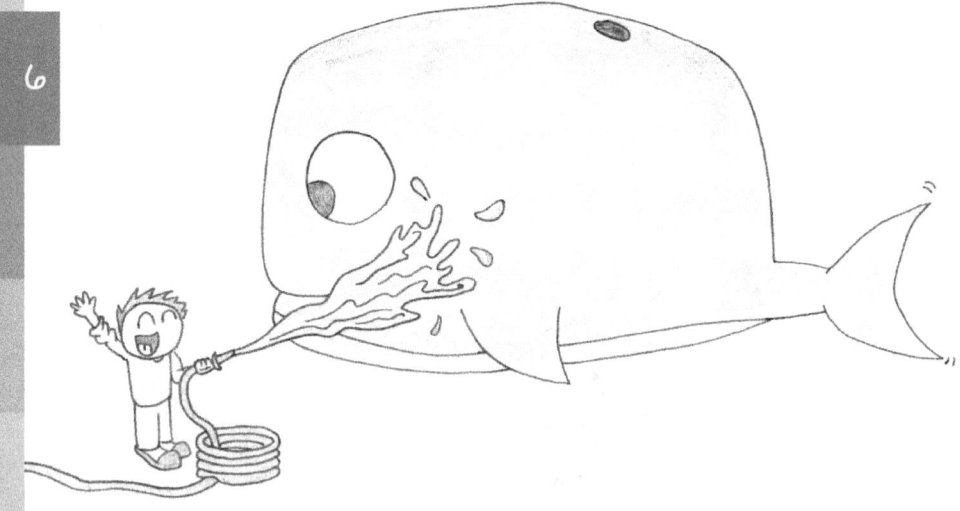

. . . What the Internet does not mention is that you have to hose them down every 15 minutes, feed them plankton every 30 minutes and that Whales are extremely loud and take up a lot of room. But you have to admit, Freckles is really cute, isn't she?

The Excuse Encyclopedia

40. THE FLY EXCUSE

I can't sleep because a fly is buzzing around my room . . .

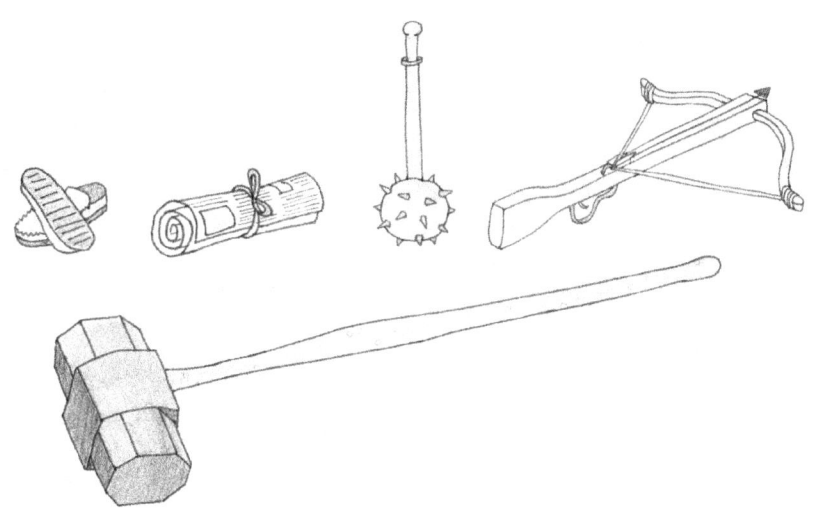

. . . you are going to have to kill it for me. That's right, if you want me to go to bed you will have to become a fly murderer. Choose your weapon wisely.

Book 6: Bedtime Excuses

41. THE ENTREPRENEUR EXCUSE

Mum, Dad, I am now a successful entrepreneur...

... This is my business - *The Online Lemonade Stand*. I sell homemade lemonade online. Now if you'll excuse me I've got deliveries to make to Mr. Perkins in London, Mrs. Xing in Shanghai and then I am going to climb to the top of Everest to open the very first mountain-top lemonade stand. Wish me luck.

The Excuse Encyclopedia

42. THE SPEECH EXCUSE

Before I go to bed I need to tell you something...

...I decided to write it all down on these cue cards so that I didn't forget anything. Hope you are sitting comfortably.

Book 6: Bedtime Excuses

43. THE BAKING EXCUSE

Don't disturb me, I'm in the middle of baking you a delicious cake . . .

. . . The next step in the recipe book says to put the cake in the oven for 97 minutes, which just so happens to be the exact running time for my new DVD. You go put the film on and I'll go get the popcorn.

44. THE NOISE EXCUSE

Ok, time for bed. Good ni . . . wait, did you hear a noise . . .

. . . It sounded like there is something outside? You'd better go investigate . . . *Then follow your parent down the stairs, lock the door behind them and get comfortable on the sofa in front of the TV.*

Book 6: Bedtime Excuses

45. THE MONSTERS EXCUSE

I'm scared! Please check my bedroom for monsters before I go to bed . . . But before you go in there, these are the monsters you are looking for:

YOUR BIG ANGRY BOSS **THE TAX-MAN** **THE ADULT-SNATCHER**

1. Your Big Angry Boss (who yells at you for no reason).
2. The Tax-Man (he's been looking for you, something about *overdue taxes*.
3. The Adult-Snatcher (snatches fully grown humans and locks them in his dungeon).

Don't worry if you're as scared as I am. Maybe we could stay up all night together?

The Excuse Encyclopedia

46. THE NOCTURNAL EXCUSE

Go to sleep, now? But I've just woken up . . .

. . . Did I forget to tell you I am *nocturnal* now? It means that I go to bed in the daytime and stay awake at night. My bedtime is now 8am, not 8pm. I had a relaxing day's sleep at school and now it's time to get all my jobs done.

47. THE FRIDGE BED EXCUSE

My bed is extremely uncomfortable. I always wake up with backache...

... So I decided I would give the fridge a try. I had to make room for my pillow and all my teddies. I hope you don't mind.

48. THE NIGHTMARE EXCUSE

But I can't go to sleep, Dad. If I do then the big, nasty crocodile will eat me . . .

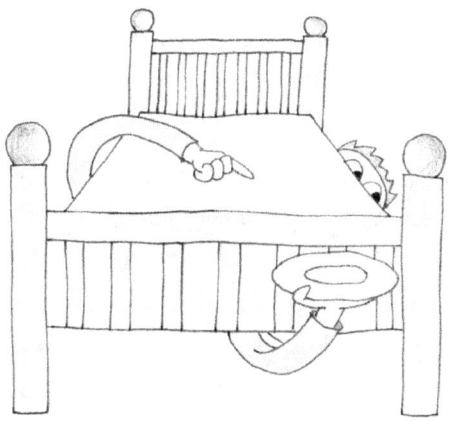

. . . I have the same terrifying nightmare every night. Perhaps if you made me a peanut butter sandwich I could give it to the crocodile and we'll become friends.

Book 6: Bedtime Excuses

49. THE UP-SALE EXCUSE

I know that my bedtime time is normally 9pm, but . . .

. . . if I do all my homework on time, tidy my bedroom, wash the car at the weekend and only read my books after 9pm could I stay up till 10pm tonight?

Smile sweetly, enlarge your eyeballs, and don't forget to say please!

BONUS: ALLERGIC EXCUSE

I definitely need to go have a lie down . . .

. . . Why? This might seem like I am overreacting, but I think I am having an allergic reaction to you telling me to 'tidy my bedroom'. I better go and lie on the sofa for the next four hours and watch cartoons.

Book 6: Bedtime Excuses

BONUS: FACEBOOK FRIEND EXCUSE

Dad. I've a deal to make with you . . .

. . . If you tidy my bedroom and tell Mum that I did it, I'll one day do you the honour and privilege of adding you as my Facebook friend.

The Excuse Encyclopedia

BONUS: READ ALL NIGHT EXCUSE

I love going to bed on time. Night, night . . .

. . . By the way, we need more AA batteries for my torch and I'll need to go to the library tomorrow morning.

Book 6: Bedtime Excuses

BONUS: SHOOTING STAR EXCUSE

My science teacher told us we have to stay up really late tonight...

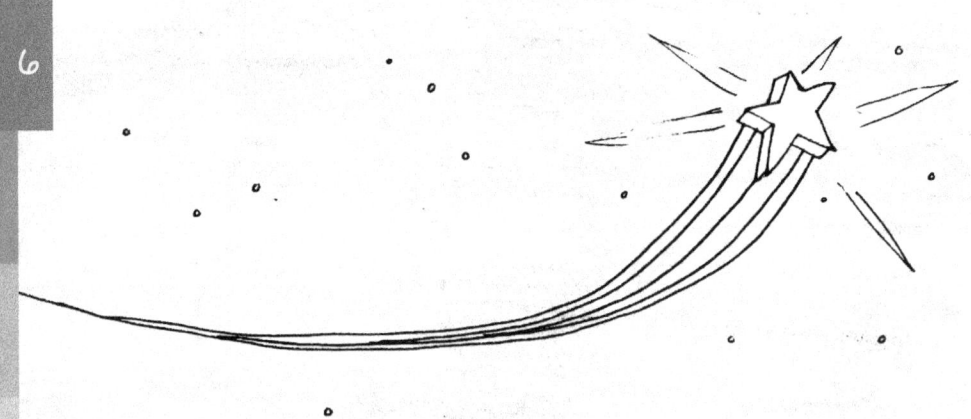

... Why? Because if you let me stay up past my bedtime tonight we could see shooting stars. And if we do see any I promise I'll make an unselfish wish.

The Excuse Encyclopedia

BONUS: AIRING CUPBOARD EXCUSE

Bad news. Someone has stolen my duvet. . .

. . . And not just mine. Every single duvet in the house has disappeared so no one will be able to go to bed! Don't bother checking the airing cupboard, I've already checked there.

Book 6: Bedtime Excuses

BONUS: HOT COCOA EXCUSE

I CANNOT go to sleep until I've had hot cocoa...

... Remember, it has to have mini-marshmallows, hand whipped cream and chocolate shavings (all made by a professional French Chocolatier).

BONUS: EVIL FART EXCUSE

I can't go to bed . . .

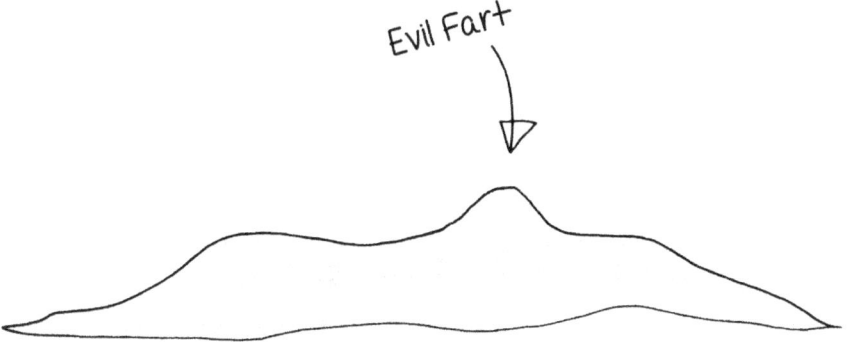

. . . My older brother has left an evil fart under my duvet (and it's waiting for me).

Book 6: Bedtime Excuses

BONUS: THE MYSTERY SCREW EXCUSE

I'm sure it's nothing, and I'm just being paranoid but . . .

. . . I found this extremely important looking screw under my bed. And it does feel a little on the wobbly side. Maybe I should sleep on the sofa, just for tonight.

BONUS: THE PILLOW OF DOOM EXCUSE

I'm terrified of my pillow...

... Don't laugh. It's a real fear. If I go to sleep it will rise up and destroy all civilisation. Don't worry, though, as I'm going to stay up and stand guard.

Book 6: Bedtime Excuses

BONUS: NEVER, EVER SLEEP EXCUSE

The Bogeyman, the Grinch, and the Wicked Witch of the West . . .

. . . None of them sleep. And so, therefore, neither do I.

BONUS: TOO HOT EXCUSE

Seriously, it's way too HOT to go to sleep tonight . . .

. . . In fact, it's too hot to do anything (except eat ice cream).

Book 6: Bedtime Excuses

BONUS: FACEBOOK THREAT EXCUSE

If you let me stay up late tonight . . .

. . . I promise I will never tell anyone that your life is not as awesome as you pretend it is on Facebook.

The Excuse Encyclopedia

BONUS: TOO COLD EXCUSE

Seriously, it's way too cold to go to sleep . . .

. . . I need twenty hot water bottles, a hug from a friendly yeti and a massive mug of hot chocolate before I can go to bed.

Excuses for Being Really Late

Book 7: Late Excuses

1. THE GOOD MORNING EXCUSE

Isn't it such a wonderful morning . . .

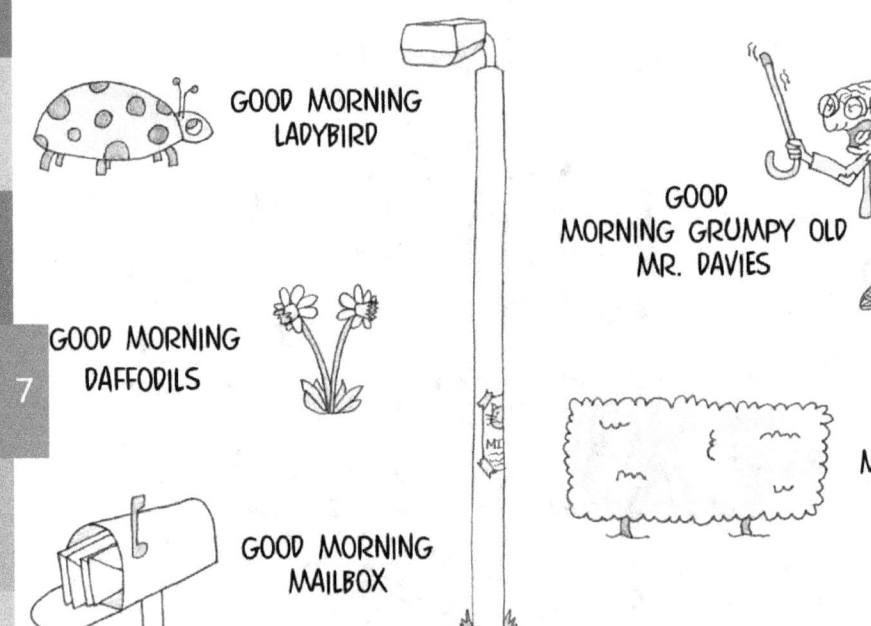

. . . I had to stop and say good morning to everything and everyone I met on my wonderful walk to school this morning.

(Once you've listed everything you can think of, finish by saying "good morning" to your teacher.)

2. THE THINKING EXCUSE

I admit to being late this morning . . .

. . . But I promise I was thinking about school the whole time.

Book 7: Late Excuses

3. THE LITTLE MISS LATE EXCUSE

Do you like my fancy dress costume...

... I'm going to a friend's birthday party as *Little Miss Late*. So I decided to put on my costume this morning and get into character.

4. THE SNOOZE BUTTON EXCUSE

Sorry I'm late. I slept in, again . . .

. . . I blame the snooze button. It always taunts me in the morning. Well, this morning I managed to defeat it once and for all! Does anyone know where I can buy an alarm clock without a snooze button?

Book 7: Late Excuses

5. THE SHORT-CUT EXCUSE

Sorry I'm late . . .

. . . That's the last time I decide to take a short-cut through the local building site!

6. THE TEN MINUTE SILENCE EXCUSE

I accidentally dropped my breakfast on the floor this morning . . .

. . . So I held a 10 minute silence in honour of this terrible tragedy and loss of nutritional life. R.I.P. jam on toast. I'll never forget you.

Book 7: Late Excuses

7. THE CAT FIGHT EXCUSE

My cat got in a fight at 2am...

...So I had to teach him a valuable lesson about waking up his owner in the early hours of the morning. I hope you'll agree that Gizmo has learnt his lesson.

The Excuse Encyclopedia

8. THE JEALOUS PILLOWS EXCUSE

Really sorry I'm late, but my pillows suffer from Separation Anxiety . . .

. . . They have grown so attached to me that they can't function as law-abiding pillows without being close to me. Now I have to take them with me everywhere I go.

Book 7: Late Excuses

9. THE WRONG BIKE EXCUSE

My bike had a flat tyre this morning, so I borrowed my mum's bike . . .

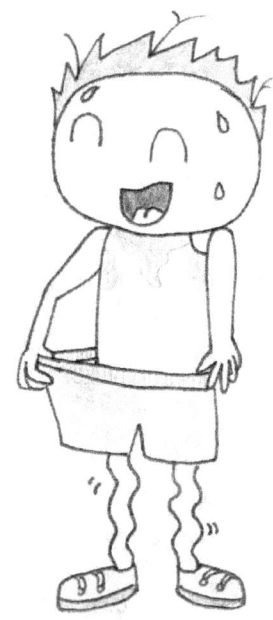

. . . After cycling 20 miles I realised it was an aerobic bike. But on the bright side I lost three pounds!

The Excuse Encyclopedia

10. THE BEAUTY SLEEP EXCUSE

Look, I know I'm late - *again* - but have you seen my face? . . .

. . . I desperately need extra beauty sleep. If you don't believe me I can get a doctor's note. My mum is a doctor and she screams and then hides behind a chair every time I walk into the room.

Book 7: Late Excuses

11. THE WONDERLAND EXCUSE

I was walking to school when I accidentally fell down a rabbit hole . . .

. . . Then I had a lovely tea party with some odd but nice people. Yes, I did just read Alice in Wonderland. How did you know that?

The Excuse Encyclopedia

12. THE WATCH RESET EXCUSE

What? It's 9:35am! That's odd, my watch says 8:45am...

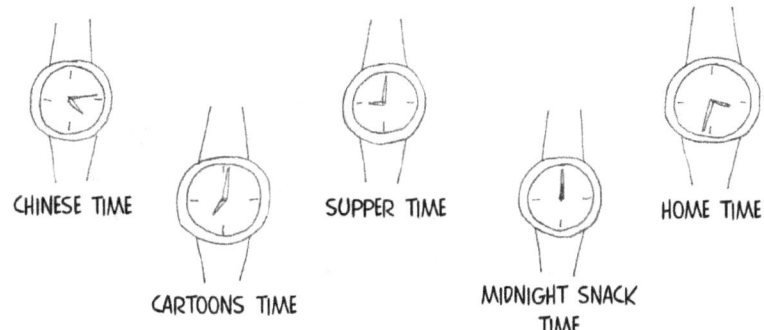

CHINESE TIME

CARTOONS TIME

SUPPER TIME

MIDNIGHT SNACK TIME

HOME TIME

...Although come to think of it I did adjust my watch forward by *8* hours to see what time it was in China, then adjust the time back to 7am so I could watch cartoons, then adjust the time forward to 9pm so I could have supper, then adjust the time forward by *3* hours so I could have a midnight snack, then adjust the time back to 3:30pm so I could pretend it was home time. What's the time again?

13. THE NEW INVENTION EXCUSE

I've invented a brand new mode of transport. Behold! *The Solar-Powered Monster Truck* . . .

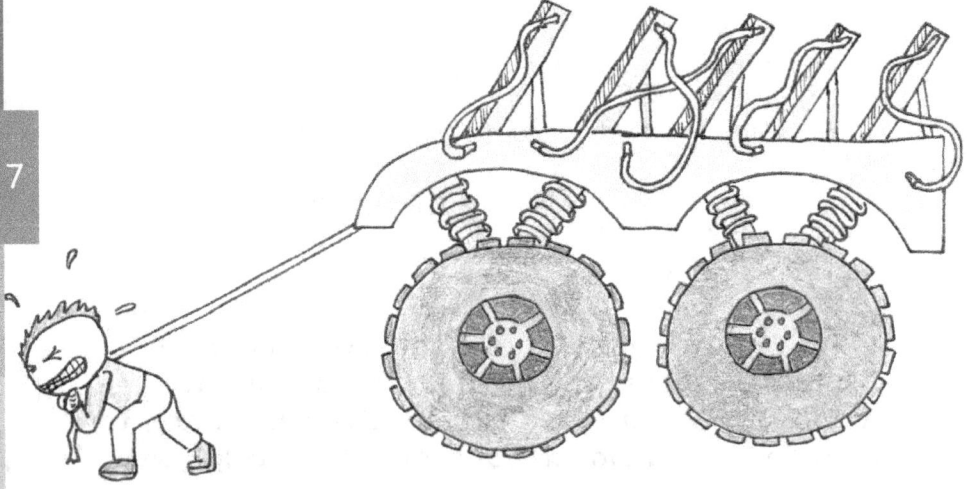

. . . Unfortunately, being solar-powered, it stopped halfway to school when it started to rain. I had to pull it the rest of the way. Maybe I could build a *Rain-Powered Monster Truck* during the Geography lesson later?

14. THE CLEAN EXCUSE

I had to have 3 showers this morning . . .

. . . Let me explain. I had my morning shower and then walked into a spider's web. Then I had another shower and then slipped on a banana skin and fell into the bin. Then I had another shower and then fell in a muddy puddle at the school entrance. But at least I'm clean.

15. THE WRONG MAP EXCUSE

The new school layout is far too confusing . . .

. . . I keep on getting lost! I think I'm in Adventureland because I've walked past Space Mountain and dodged Buzz Lightyear's Astro Blasters. I can now see Tarzan's Treehouse and the Pirate's Lair on Tom Sawyer Island in the distance. Is my new classroom in the big, fancy castle?

The Excuse Encyclopedia

16. THE NEW SHOES EXCUSE

I bought these new protective shoes . . .

. . . I didn't realise that they are made from concrete, lead and osmium (the heaviest metal in the world).

Book 7: Late Excuses

17. THE LONELY GOLDFISH EXCUSE

I just couldn't leave my house this morning . . .

. . . It's Seaweed's fault. Look at him. I'd like to see you try and leave my goldfish while he is giving you the *don't leave me again* look.

The Excuse Encyclopedia

18. THE HEADTEACHER EXCUSE

Sorry I am late, but I just had a wonderful conversation with the Headteacher...

... We discussed your career progression at this school. We both agreed that you're making good progress in the classroom and how your teaching has inspired me to become a better human being.

19. THE CAR KEYS EXCUSE

I told Lassie to bury my Dad's car keys for a prank...

... Unfortunately Lassie misunderstood the prank and buried the car instead. She's an extremely obedient dog, pretty stupid, but obedient none the less.

20. THE FASHIONABLE EXCUSE

When I grow up I want to work in the fashion industry...

...Haven't you heard of being *fashionably late?* This is all good practise for my future career. I'll see you again at a fashionable time tomorrow.

Book 7: Late Excuses

21. THE NEW WORKOUT EXCUSE

I'm trying to get fit, so I tried a new workout . . .

. . . I get dropped off 5 miles away from school with 5 minutes to go. I'm exhausted, I need to lie down.

The Excuse Encyclopedia

22. THE TOAD KISSING EXCUSE

Sorry I'm late, but I had to give it a go . . .

. . . My dad read *The Princess & the Toad* to me last night so I spent all morning looking for my Prince. If you are wondering whether I found him, then the answer is no.

23. THE BREAKFEAST EXCUSE

My mum says that breakfast is the most important meal of the day . . .

. . . So I made sure I ate as much as I could this morning; I had a *breakFEAST*. It took me a while to roll all the way to school, which I personally think should not have been built on a hill.

24. THE WRONG SPECTACLES EXCUSE

My dad has terrible eyesight, and my eyesight is even worse...

... So this morning my dad accidentally took my glasses to work. Which meant that I had to walk to school wearing his glasses! Am I in the right class?

25. THE CAR SWAP EXCUSE

I decided to use my brother's car to get to school this morning . . .

. . . My little brother's car has 2 leg power, 4" plastic alloys and is extremely energy efficient.

26. THE LATE DAY EXCUSE

But don't you know? Did nobody tell you? .
. .

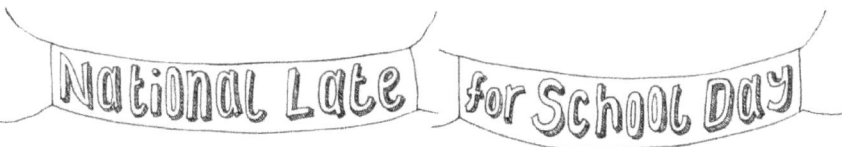

. . . It's *National Late for School Day!*

27. THE DANCING SHOES EXCUSE

I decided to wear my tap dancing shoes to walk to school today...

... I accidentally tap danced my way into an audition for the local production of *Hairspray the Musical* and have been given the lead role of Tracy Turnblad. By the way, rehearsals are 7am - 10am for the next 8 weeks.

The Excuse Encyclopedia

28. THE HOME TUTOR EXCUSE

Did my parents forget to tell you, I'm being home-schooled . . .

. . . From 6am to 9am my tutor, Professor Charles Einstein Shakespeare, teaches me advanced mathematics and quantum physics. What did I miss? The six times tables? I think I'll be fine then.

Book 7: Late Excuses

29. THE PRESENT EXCUSE

Sorry I am late, but there was a queue at the Flower Shop . . .

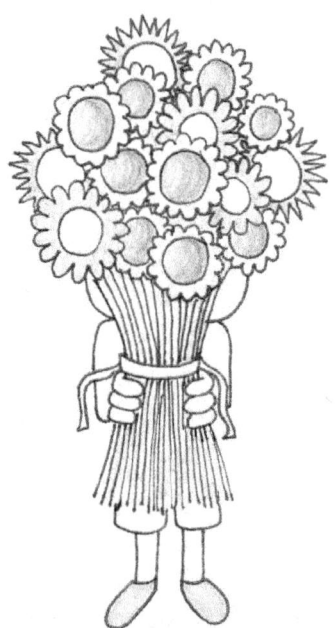

. . . I bought them to apologise for being late to class yesterday. I guess I'll have to buy an even bigger bunch of flowers tomorrow morning.

30. THE BUMP ON THE HEAD EXCUSE

I bumped my head when I woke up this morning . . .

. . . My mum told me that when I bump my head I should lie down for 5 minutes. Maybe I should stop sleeping in a bunk bed.

31. THE HELPING OTHERS EXCUSE

Well, this time I was late for purely unselfish reasons...

... I helped an old lady cross the road, I saved a cat from a tree and I deweeded the school garden. If there is anything else I can help you with let me know and I'll do it tomorrow morning.

The Excuse Encyclopedia

32. THE HYPOCHONDRIAC EXCUSE

I'm feeling very well this morning . . .

. . . So well, in fact, that something *MUST* be wrong! Don't panic though. I did an extremely thorough 3 hour diagnostic test on myself this morning and, good news, I'm as healthy as a celery stick.

Book 7: Late Excuses

33. THE HOMEWORK EXCUSE

I was halfway to school when I realised I forgot my art homework . . .

. . . I spent all weekend working on it. I had to go back to get it. It's my design for a new school building made entirely of matchsticks and chewing gum.

34. THE DOG WALKING EXCUSE

I decided to take the dog for a morning stroll before school . . .

. . . When I got back my hamster looked jealous, so I took him for a roll about. Then when I got back the goldfish looked jealous, so I took him for a walk on the skateboard. Then when I got back my pyjamas looked jealous, so I put them back on and had a quick snooze.

Book 7: Late Excuses

35. THE LOST EXCUSE

I took a different route to school this morning . . .

. . . I did get very very lost, but I did walk past a flower shop, a card shop and a big cuddly bear shop. These are for you.

36. THE SUBWAY EXCUSE

The subway made me late...

...By that I mean the subway train was late, not that I was stuck in a queue at Subway ordering a foot-long sub.

Book 7: Late Excuses

37. THE EARLY BIRD EXCUSE

Wait, before you tell me that I am late . .

. . . I am actually really, really early for tomorrow. See, I brought my geography, history and maths books ready for tomorrow's lessons.

38. THE OPPOSITES ATTRACT EXCUSE

I am looking for a boyfriend who is intelligent, has wonderful hair, and is always on time . . .

. . . My mum told me that 'opposites attract'. So I've stopped doing my homework, combing my hair, and started to turn up late for everything. By the way I've got a Dentist Appointment at 2pm so I'll need to leave class at 2:30pm sharp.

Book 7: Late Excuses

39. THE BIRTHDAY EXCUSE

I know I'm late, but I had to celebrate. Today is his 1st birthday...

...Happy Birthday Angus! My pet hamster's birthday wish was to spend the day with me and I granted it.

40. THE DROP OFF EXCUSE

Sorry I'm late, I was dropping my parents off at work . . .

. . . The traffic was awful this morning on the 'work-run'. I'm thinking I should invest in better transportation. How about a catapult?

41. THE BROKEN WATCH EXCUSE

Have you seen the weather outside? . . .

. . . It's cloudy. My brand new watch is solar-powered which unfortunately means it only works in sunlight. Could someone tell me the time please? How late am I?

The Excuse Encyclopedia

42. THE FROG-I-CORN EXCUSE

I was searching for a Frog-i-corn...

... Have you heard *the legend of the Frog-i-corn?* They are half-frog, half-unicorn. They hide in children's bedrooms. They only eat lucky charms. And if you manage to catch a Frog-i-corn they'll grant you one wish.

Book 7: Late Excuses

43. THE NOT-SO-LATE EXCUSE

I don't mean to be rude, but . . .

. . . According to my watch it seems to me that everyone else was early this morning.

44. THE TIME EXCUSE

Look at all of you idiots, scurrying about like little ants . . .

. . . Not me, I've seen the light. *Time is an illusion.* I have found the key to unlocking the handcuffs of the mind. Join me, and you too can be free from the sands of time.

45. THE SNAIL CROSSING EXCUSE

Have you heard of the latest eco-friendly scheme . . .

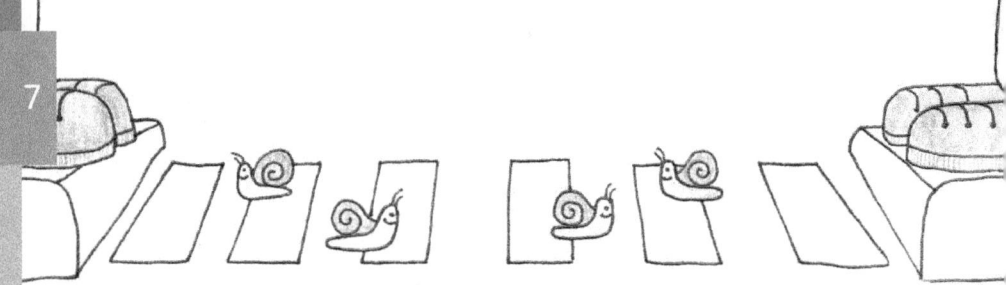

. . . The council have made this snail crossing on the cyclepath. I was waiting for 15 minutes for a family of snails this morning, but I'm glad the snails can cross the path without the fear of being squished.

46. THE LOST MY GLASSES EXCUSE

I couldn't find my glasses this morning . .

. . . Which then meant I got on the wrong number bus, went to the wrong school and spent the morning learning how to make a pottery bowl.

Book 7: Late Excuses

47. THE LATE PASS EXCUSE

Late? I know I'm late, and here's your proof...

... It's my late pass. The Headteacher gave it to me. It's a new school scheme for forgetful pupils, like me

The Excuse Encyclopedia

48. THE GRIEVING EXCUSE

Sorry, I've had an emotional morning . . .

. . . I was at my friend's grandad's brother's granddaughter's neighbour's pet fish's funeral. Yes, it was very tragic.

Book 7: Late Excuses

49. THE RUN-OUT EXCUSE

I've officially run out of excuses . . .

. . . So therefore I, [insert your name here], apologise for my lateness and I promise to try my best to get to school earlier tomorrow.

Tips to help you get to school early:
1. Set your watch 10 minutes fast
2. Buy a jetpack
3. Brush your teeth in the shower
4. Invent a time machine
5. Get up earlier

BONUS: SAVING YOUR PET EXCUSE

I know I'm really late, but I had to save my pet goldfish...

... It may have looked like she was fine to the average pet owner, but I knew that Cassie the goldfish was either drowning or overdosing on water. I'll now have to go take her to the vet right away.

Book 7: Late Excuses

BONUS: TAKE OUT EXCUSE

I fancied an authentic Chinese takeaway . . .

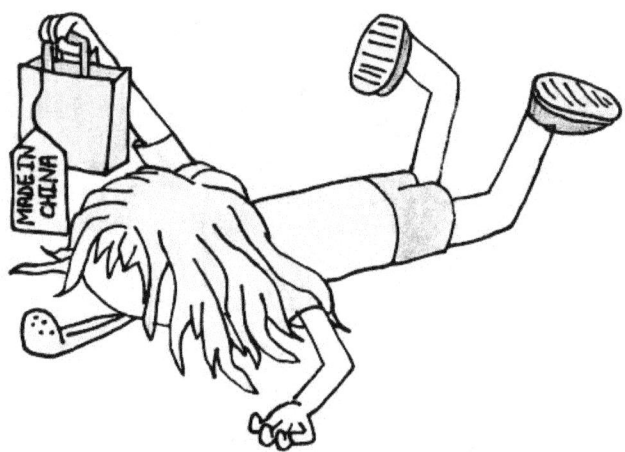

. . . Do you know how far away China is? It was a 8,500 mile trip! So, what have I missed over the past two months?

BONUS: SICK BED EXCUSE

My bed told me that it was feeling very sick this morning . . .

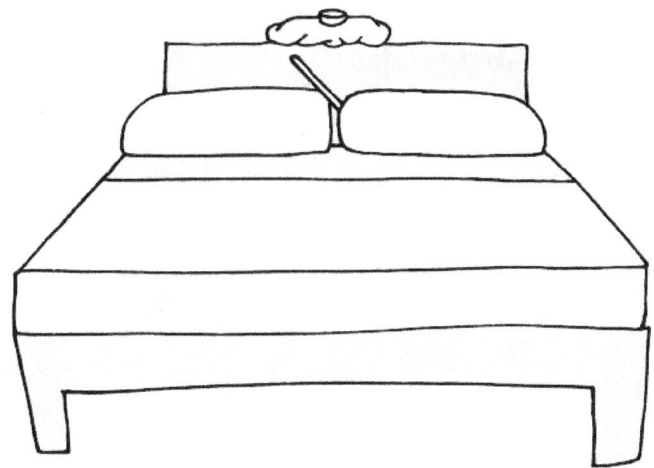

. . . So, I had to stay home and look after it.

Book 7: Late Excuses

BONUS: IMPORTANT SEMINAR EXCUSE

I know that I'm late, again . . .

. . . but I want you to know it was because I was attending a seminar called 'How to Organise Your Time So That You Are Never Late Again'.

The Excuse Encyclopedia

BONUS: BUTTERFLY EXCUSE

Erm, why am I late? . . .

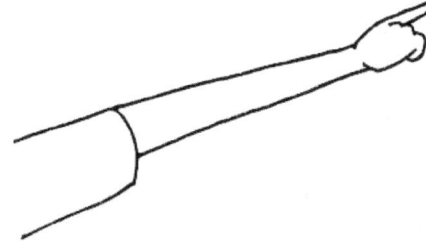

. . . Well, you know the butterfly flapping it's wings thing? That's why I'm late.

Book 7: Late Excuses

BONUS: LAZY SLOB EXCUSE

It may look like I don't care . . .

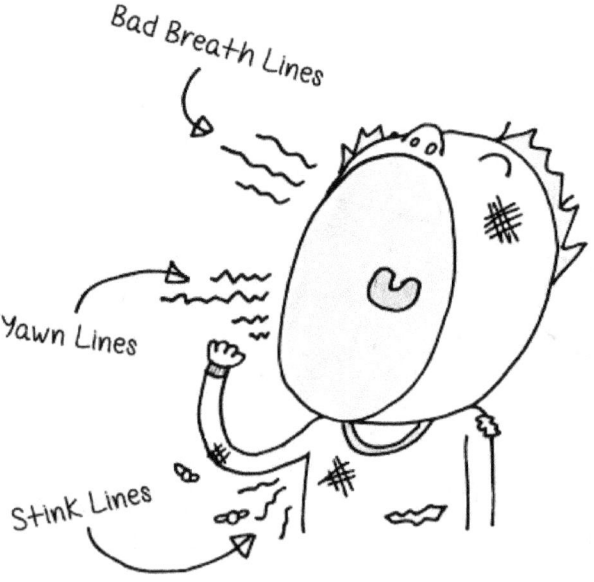

Bad Breath Lines

Yawn Lines

Stink Lines

. . . But I am trying extremely hard to be a living, breathing and smelly example to how your life could have turned out to be much, much worse.

BONUS: HARRY 'LATE FOR CLASS' POTTER EXCUSE

Ahhh drat! I was hoping that if I turned up late for class dressed as Harry Potter...

... you, my favourite teacher, would transfigure from a cat into Professor McGonagall and then threaten to turn me into pocket watch. I'll have to try it with all the other teachers as well, of course.

Book 7: Late Excuses

BONUS: TREE EXCUSE

Erm, why am I late? . . .

. . . Well, you know the tree falling in the woods thing? That's why I'm late.

BONUS: TOOTHBRUSH ACCIDENT EXCUSE

I'm sorry for being late but I had to go to hospital . . .

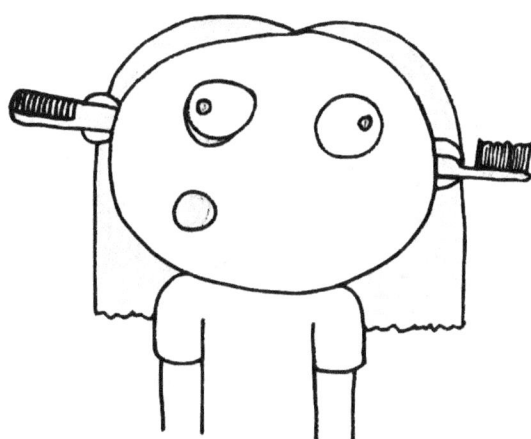

. . . After a sleepless night I kept missied my mouth when brushing my teeth this morning. The doctors said that they can't remove the toothbrush without causing permanent brain damage, but on the bright side my ears are minty-fresh and plaque-free.

Book 7: Late Excuses

BONUS: IMAGINARY FRIEND EXCUSE

It's not me who is late, it's my imaginary friend . . .

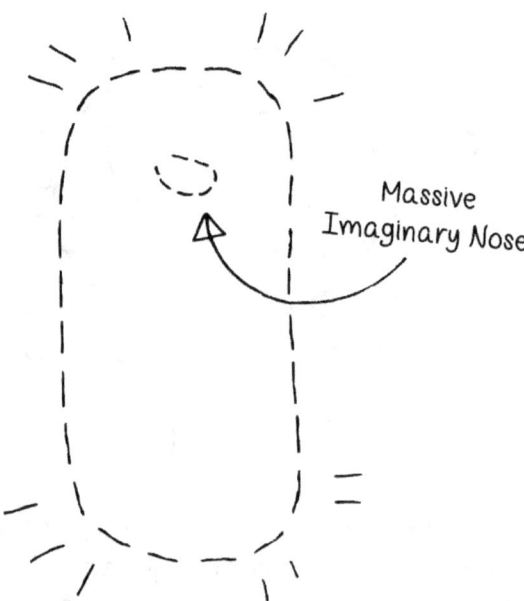

Massive Imaginary Nose

. . . It took her one hour and thirty minutes to powder her nose this morning. Don't worry, I'll have words with her.

BONUS: RAT TRAPS EXCUSE

I'm sorry for being late, but this one is a great excuse...

...An army of ants moved into my bedroom over the weekend. Pest Control have come and covered the whole house with rat traps so it took me a long time to navigate my way to the front door.

Book 7: Late Excuses

BONUS: EMAILS EXCUSE

I was late to school this morning for a very good reason...

...As you can see I currently have 271 new emails. I started the morning with 2,389 emails. I really need to unsubscribe from some of the marketing email lists.

BONUS: POOL EXCUSE

Hang on . . .

. . . I thought you said we were meeting at the 'pool', instead of 'school'. Anyone got a change of clothes?

BONUS: EMPTY TANK EXCUSE

I was late because the car run out of fuel . . .

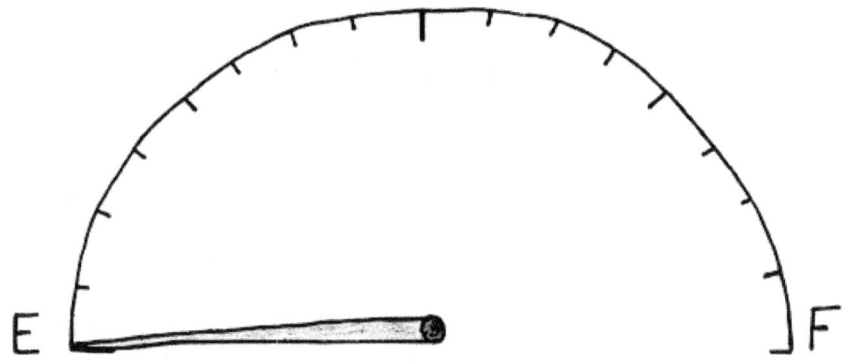

. . . Turns out the 'F' stands for 'Full' and not 'Fast-Mode' and the 'E' stands for 'Empty' and not 'Eco-Mode'.

7

BOOK EIGHT

Excuses for Not Eating Your Vegetables

VEGETABLE EXCUSES

Book 8: Vegetable Excuses

1. THE DECAYING EXCUSE

Did you know vegetables are perishable? .

. . . When cooked, vegetables will decay and go mouldy after 2-3 days. On the other hand, puddings will decay and go mouldy after 5-7 days. So in answer to your statement - *"you can't eat pudding until you've eaten your greens"* - I think I'll wait at the dinner table for the next 4 days and see what happens.

2. THE VEG-TABLE EXCUSE

The school nurse has diagnosed me with a severe allergy to veg . . .

. . . Bizarrely, I'm also mildly allergic to tables. Which means that if you ever put vegetables on a table I am sitting at I will die a horrible death. Honestly, it's quite a lethal combination!

3. THE FRUIT & VEG EXCUSE

Did you know that potatos are actually *root vegetables*? . . .

. . . And tomatos are actually *fruit*. So from now on I recommend you serve chips and tomato sauce with every single meal, so that I am always eating my fruit and vegetables.

4. THE HAMSTER EXCUSE

I've been inspired by Hammy my pet Hamster...

... I'm going to store my vegetables in my massive cheeks for later. Now then, please excuse me while I go to the bathroom to powder my nose.

5. THE HUNGRY BIN EXCUSE

Look, the poor little kitchen bin is hungry . . .

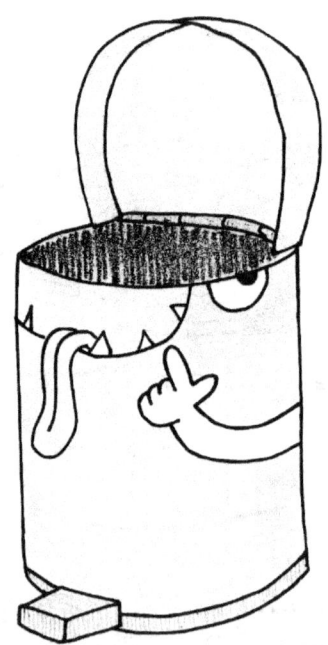

. . . I was going to eat all my yummy sprouts but seeing as I am such a thoughtful young lady I've decided to donate them. Don't worry, kitchen bin, I'll never let you go hungry again.

6. THE MOUSTACHE EXCUSE

Have you heard of Movember? . . .

. . . Men all over the world grow a moustache to raise awareness for Men's Health and I've joined them. Unfortunately I will not be able to squeeze vegetables through my magnificent moustache for a whole month, but it's for a worthy cause.

Book 8: Vegetable Excuses

7. THE LOCK JAW EXCUSE

Em fmm shmmm phm! . . . .

. . . Shmmm chmm brm thmmy wm qumm glm.

8. THE TASTE BUDS EXCUSE

Look, here is my tongue map . . .

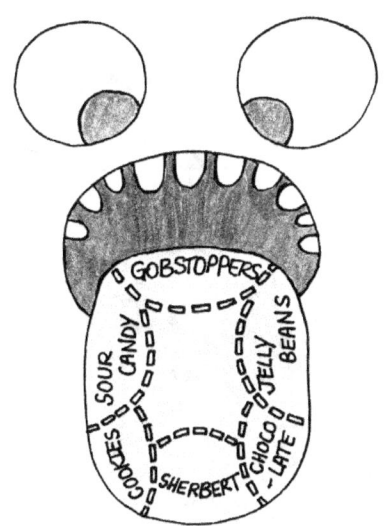

. . . As you can clearly see, my adolescent tongue has not yet developed the taste buds to fully appreciate the complex flavours of vegetables.

Book 8: Vegetable Excuses

9. THE AFRICA EXCUSE

I saw an advert on the TV yesterday . . .

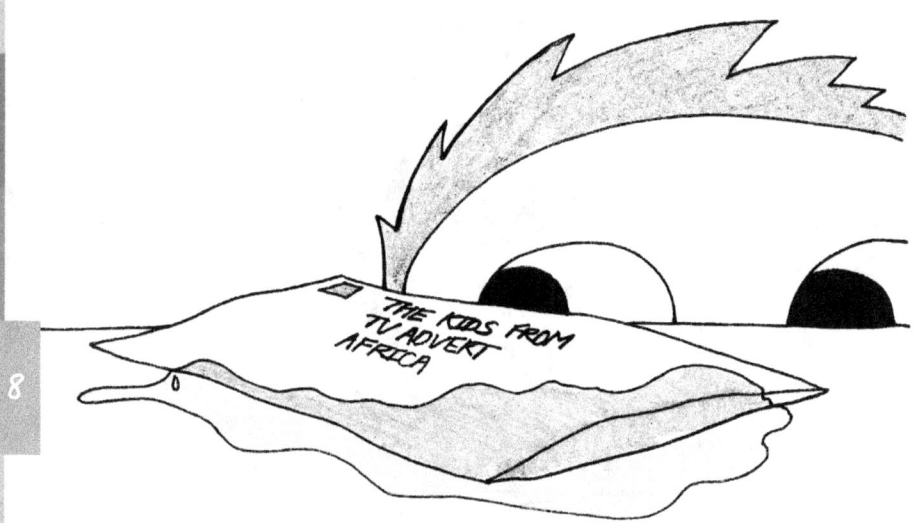

. . . Did you know there are millions of children in Africa going to bed hungry every single day? So, out of the kindness of my heart, I've decided to make a charitable donation.

The Excuse Encyclopedia

10. THE MULTI-STOMACH EXCUSE

I've done extensive research into the digestive system of children...

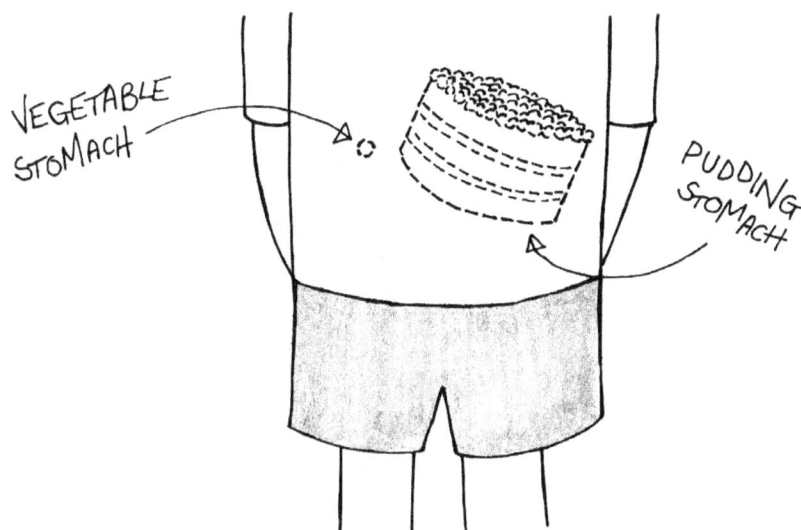

... I have discovered something that will change dinner time forever. Children under the age of *[insert your age, plus a few years, here]* have two stomachs: one for vegetables the size of a garden pea, the other for pudding the size of a large chocolate cake.

Book 8: Vegetable Excuses

11. THE PUDDITARIAN EXCUSE

You know Auntie Rebecca? . . .

. . . She is a vegetarian. I've been doing a lot of thinking and she has inspired me to become a *pudditarian*. So from now on I only eat puddings.

The Excuse Encyclopedia

12. THE NEGOTIATIONS EXCUSE

Sure, I'll eat my vegetables . . .

. . . If you do one of the following things for me: burn down my school, transform my rabbit into a T-Rex, or move the orbit of the earth in a single jump.

Book 8: Vegetable Excuses

13. THE REWARD CHART EXCUSE

You know how I really struggle to eat my vegetables...

VEGETABLE REWARD CHART	
Days eating his Veggies	The Reward
1	Trip to Disneyland
2	Trip to the Moon
3	One-way trip to the centre of the Earth (for my big sister)

...Well I decided to make a reward chart to help me. I'll need you to sign the bottom, as it's a legally binding contract.

14. THE MUSICAL EXCUSE

Scientists think that music makes food taste better...

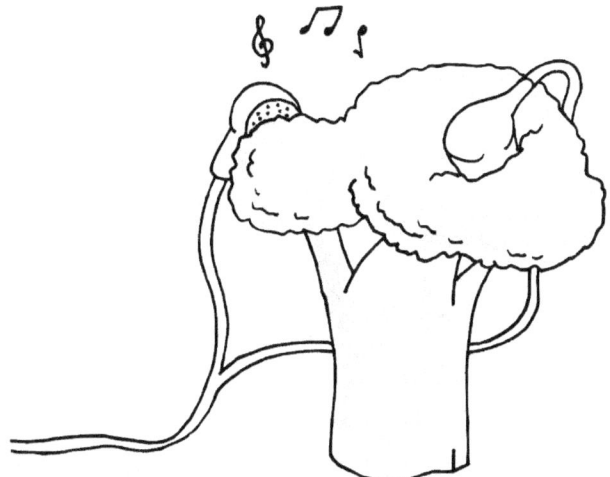

...Seeing as this piece of broccoli tastes absolutely disgusting I've made an eight hour long playlist for it to listen to.

Book 8: Vegetable Excuses

15. THE DINNER WITCH EXCUSE

I've got to leave all my vegetables tonight . . .

. . . On *[insert date here]* every year the Dinner Witch visits and if you don't leave her vegetable offerings she will turn you into an ugly little toad with an embarrassing haircut.

16. THE PIZZA EXCUSE

Behold! The only food I need to eat for the rest of my life...

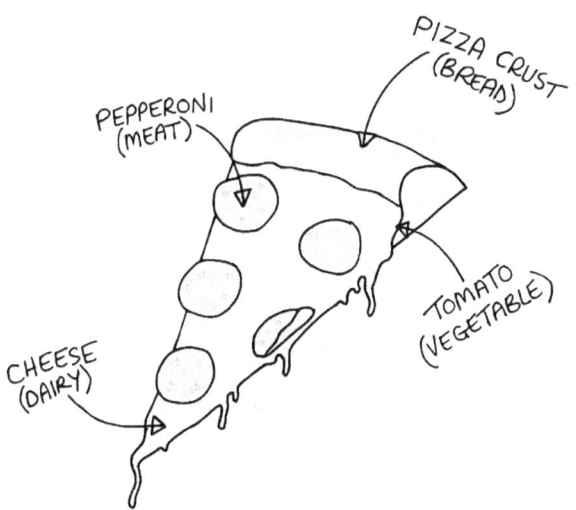

... PIZZA! This magical wonder food contains every food group, including vegetables. It's a nutritional and healthy slice of pure happiness.

Book 8: Vegetable Excuses

17. THE CATAPULT EXCUSE

I've invented a new, ground-breaking method of feeding yourself...

... I call it – *The Vegetable Catapult*. Admittedly my new invention is still in the testing phase. I'll make some minor adjustments and commence the 2nd round of testing at dinner tomorrow.

18. THE DISTRACTION EXCUSE

Right, I'm going to eat my vegetables now. Are you ready? . . .

. . . WOOOOOOOOOOOOOOOOOOOOOW, WHAT IS THAT IN THE WINDOW BEHIND YOU!?! Did you not see that? I can't believe you missed it. On the bright side, I did manage to eat all my vegetables.

Book 8: Vegetable Excuses

19. THE OPEN DOOR EXCUSE

Oh no, did you leave the front door open?
. . .

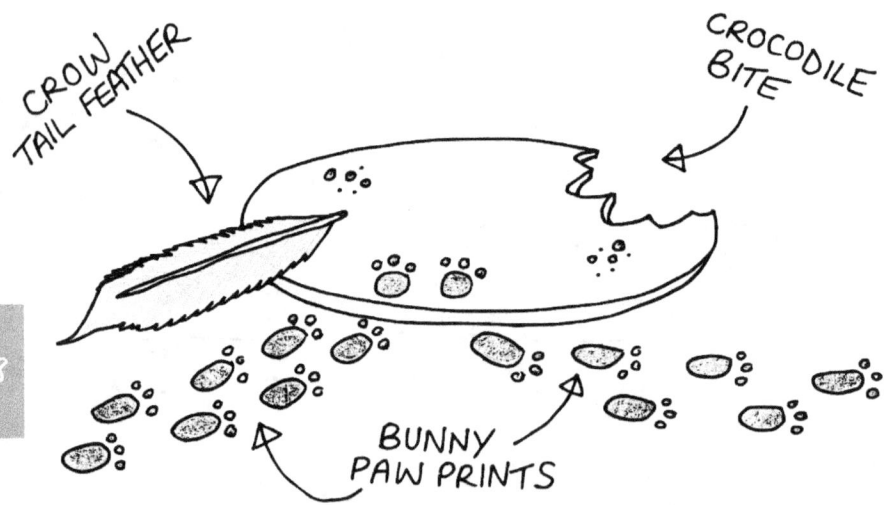

. . . Wild animals have stolen my precious vegetables. A crow stole my peas and a rabbit stole my carrots. Did you know that an alligator's favourite food is Brussels sprouts? Well, you do now.

The Excuse Encyclopedia

20. THE ALL-IN-ONE PILL EXCUSE

Behold! The All-In-One Pill . . .

. . . It contains everything the human body needs in one tiny capsule. So I don't need to eat my vegetables anymore. I know it looks like a Tic-Tac and tastes like a Tic-Tac, but I assure you, it is not a Tic-Tac.

Book 8: Vegetable Excuses

21. THE BLENDER DIET EXCUSE

I've decided to go on the *Blender Diet*...

...From now on I require all my vegetables to be blended into a smoothie. According to Dr. Snozzcumber, the food scientist behind the *Blender Diet*, they should also be mixed with two scoops of vanilla ice cream, three meringue nests and six tablespoons of sugar.

22. THE BRACES EXCUSE

I'm back from the dentist, she said to read you this letter...

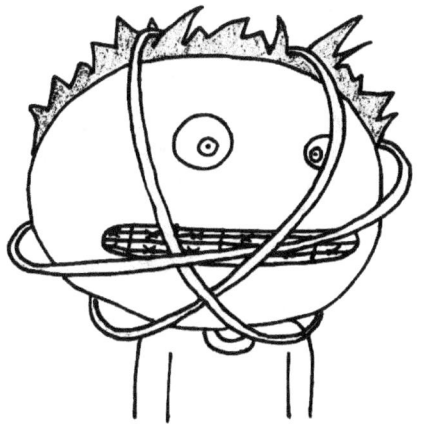

... [Open fake letter and read aloud]

Dear Parents. I am writing to inform you that the braces your son has been fitted with have an unfortunate manufacturing fault. If healthy food comes into contact with the braces it they will dissolve and all his teeth will fall out. P.S. I recommend feeding him fries covered in tomato ketchup and fizzy pop.

Book 8: Vegetable Excuses

23. THE OBSTACLE COURSE EXCUSE

Fine, I'll open wide for the airplane to land . . .

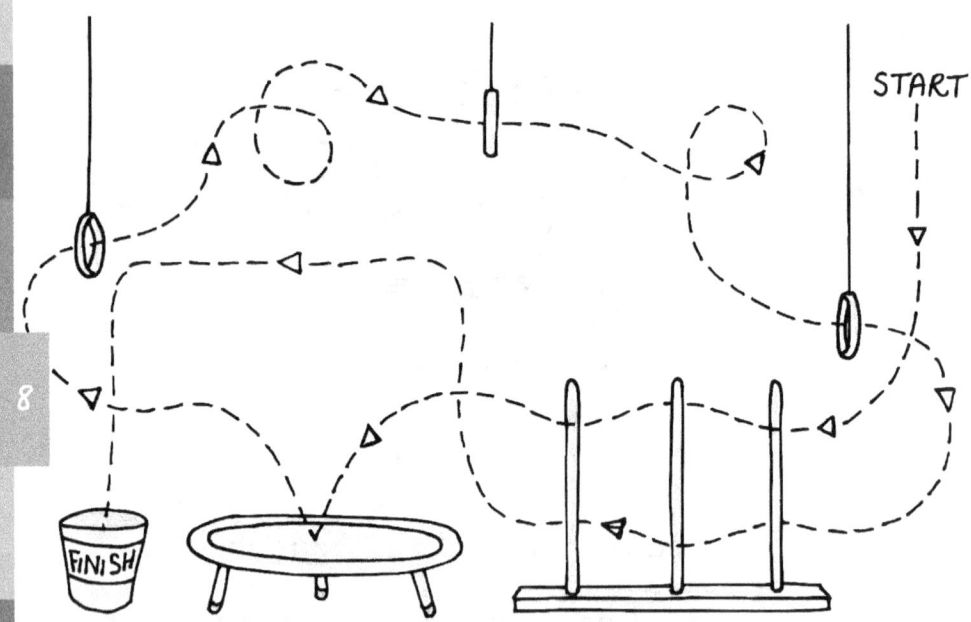

. . . But only if the pilot is able to complete this obstacle course. I do hope the vegetable pilot has a seatbelt on that plane of his.

The Excuse Encyclopedia

24. THE SUPERSTARS EXCUSE

Hang on, I recognise these guys . . .

. . . OMG! They're film stars. The tomato is called Bob, the cucumber is called Larry and this little one is called Junior Asparagus. I can't eat them!

Book 8: Vegetable Excuses

25. THE SCALES EXCUSE

Good News! I've been cast as Oliver in our school production of Oliver Twist...

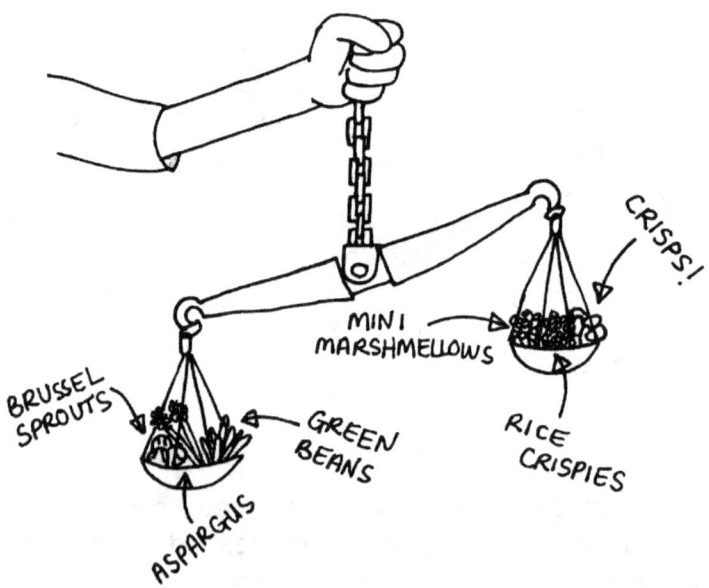

... It's a soprano part, so I will have to sing very high notes. My Drama Teacher has given me a strict diet of light and airy foods to keep my vocal chords healthy. No heavy vegetables for me.

The Excuse Encyclopedia

26. THE SNAIL POLICE EXCUSE

A snail has stolen my cabbage . . .

. . . Don't worry. I've called the Snail Police and they're already giving chase to the perpetrator. Should have my cabbage back in 3-5 days.

Book 8: Vegetable Excuses

27. THE DIRTY HANDS EXCUSE

I was going to eat my vegetables but my hands were dirty...

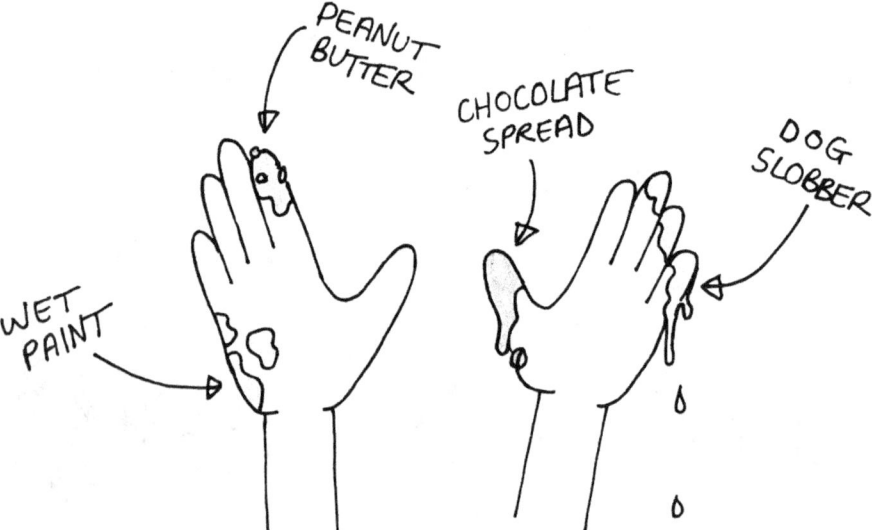

... So I washed my hands but then slipped and touched wet paint. I washed them again only for the dog to lick them. Then finally I washed them for a third time only to accidentally put my hands in jars of chocolate spread and peanut butter. Silly me!

28. THE CARROT VISION EXCUSE

My science experiment has gone slightly wrong...

...I ate twenty carrots at school, to test the *Carrots Help you See in the Dark* theory. Now everything is orange and I have a strange desire to burrow a hole and thump my left foot.

Book 8: Vegetable Excuses

29. THE GENETICS EXCUSE

Back from the kitchen already? . . .

. . . While you were gone I successfully genetically modified this parsnip into the shape of a chocolate bar. I will now eat my vegetables, and I shall do so with considerable pleasure.

30. THE CAULIFLOWER EXCUSE

Look! Look what's happened to my hair . .

. . . I told you I've eaten too much cauliflower. Now look at my hair, it's turned into a cauliflower. I need you to buy as much cheese as you can, melt it all in a big pot and slowly dip my hair in.

Book 8: Vegetable Excuses

31. THE VEGGIE COMA EXCUSE

[Leave this letter at the end of your bed]

...

... Dear [insert name here] *Parents, I've got some bad news. Your daughter has slipped into a vegetable coma. She has eaten too many vegetables. I recommend you spoon feed her chocolate spread until she wakes up. Yours sincerely, the Family Doctor.*

32. THE HAUNTED EXCUSE

Don't go down the vegetable aisle! . . .

. . . It's been closed by the Paranormal Police. I read somewhere that the aisle is haunted by a poltergeist called Jack the Tripper. He trips people up while browsing for tomatoes.

Book 8: Vegetable Excuses

33. THE COOKING INSTRUCTIONS EXCUSE

Do you smell something burning? . . .

. . . Oh dear, you mean you're not meant to spit-roast vegetables on an open fire for twenty hours?

The Excuse Encyclopedia

34. THE MAIL ORDER VEG EXCUSE

I decided to order our vegetables online. . .

. . . They call it Mail Order Veg. I think it is a fantastic idea. Unfortunately our letter box doesn't agree, and neither does the postman who decided to force the parcel through.

Book 8: Vegetable Excuses

35. THE VIRTUAL REALITY EXCUSE

But I am eating my vegetables . . .

. . . This virtual reality headset is very realistic. My virtual broccoli is a little on the chewy side, but very tasty.

36. THE ART PROJECT EXCUSE

This week's homework is to make vegetable art...

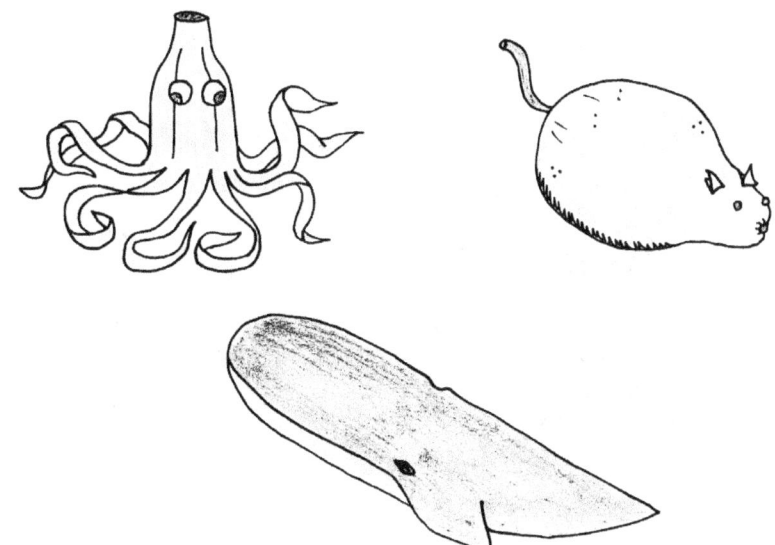

... Look at my beautiful creations. I've made an octopus from my banana, a mouse from my pear and a blue whale from my cucumber.

Book 8: Vegetable Excuses

37. THE VEG CLASS EXCUSE

Thanks for the veggies but I've already had my five-a-day...

FULL OF VEGETABLES

... There's a new lesson at school called *Veg Class*. We learned about the wonders of vegetables and ate loads of different types. This week's homework is to eat our twenty-a-week, which refers to eating a healthy variety of sweets and chocolate throughout the week.

38. THE DRUNK DRIVER EXCUSE

Stop right there! . . .

. . . I'm the Train Driver Inspector and I have reason to believe that the driver of this train is drunk at the controls. There was an anonymous tip off that this carrot has been marinating in red wine all night.

Book 8: Vegetable Excuses

39. THE PESTICIDES EXCUSE

I can't eat this carrot...

... There are pesticides all over it. Yuck! Don't worry, I'll make sure it is disposed of in a safe and humane way.

40. THE MYTH EXCUSE

Do carrots really glow in the dark? . . .

. . . Oh sorry, I got it the wrong way around. *Eating* carrots helps you see in the dark. I'm going to need three plasters and an ice pack please.

Book 8: Vegetable Excuses

41. THE MAGIC EXCUSE

Watch the Brussels sprout ...

... Tadaaaaaaa! The Brussels sprout has gone. Now I'll make the rest of my vegetables disappear too. Good boy, Fido.

The Excuse Encyclopedia

42. THE BACTERIA EXCUSE

In today's Science lesson we studied bacteria...

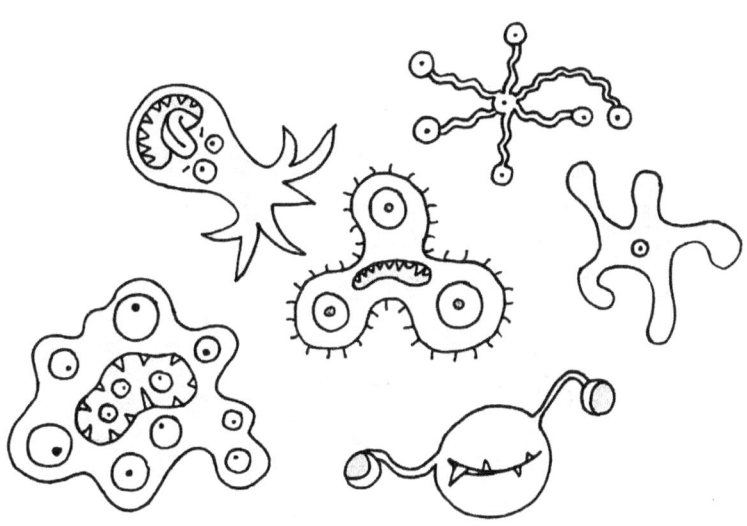

... Did you know there is good and bad bacteria? Don't worry, I've checked which kind of bacteria is on my plate of vegetables and can tell you it's all the bad kind.

Book 8: Vegetable Excuses

43. THE TASTE TESTER EXCUSE

Fido is a very good boy...

... He is my new food tester. He checks that my vegetables are not poisonous. Looks to me like today's vegetables were non-toxic, and I can tell by the way Fido is licking his lips that they were tasty too.

44. THE SETTING THE TABLE EXCUSE

Look, I set the table all by myself . . .

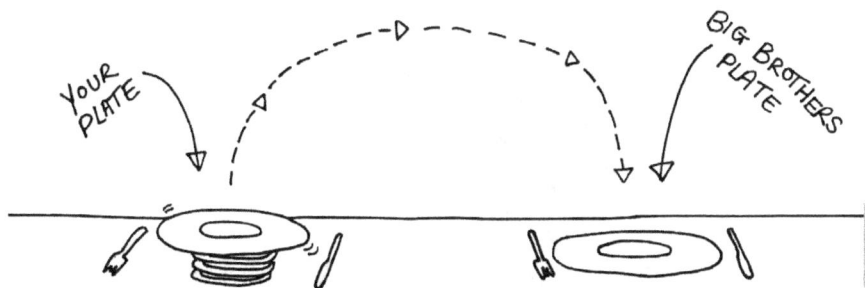

. . . I will be sitting on the left and my big brother will be sitting on the right. As you can see, my dinner plate is ready for my vegetables.

Book 8: Vegetable Excuses

45. THE BIB EXCUSE

I know that I'm a bit old for a bib now...

... It's just a precaution. I don't want any of my yummy vegetables to be wasted by falling on the floor.

46. THE GREEN EXCUSE

Oh, I almost forgot to tell you. I'm allergic to the colour green . . .

. . . I can no longer wear my Hulk fancy dress costume, use green felt tip pens or eat any green vegetables. I'm going to miss broccoli, and colouring in the bottom bits of flowers, and also hulk smashing stuff.

Book 8: Vegetable Excuses

47. THE NUTRITION EXCUSE

I've developed a new, groundbreaking eating technique...

...With the help of these state-of-the-art nutrition glasses I can soak up nutrients *with my mind*. Unfortunately the glasses only work on vegetables, so I still have to eat chocolate the traditional way.

48. THE GARDENER EXCUSE

Good news. I've become a vegetable gardener...

... I've started by burying all the vegetables that were on my plate in my new vegetable plot. In a years time we'll all have plenty of vegetables to eat. I do hope you're feeling patient.

Book 8: Vegetable Excuses

49. THE 30,000 EXCUSE

As a child I am a 'Supertaster' *[this is true, you are a supertaster]* . . .

. . . I was born with around 30,000 taste buds *[true]* which means eating bitter vegetables is a very intense experience and can be extremely difficult *[again, true]*. I'll continue to try and eat my vegetables, as I know they are good for me. And remember, once I'm an adult I'll have around 10,000 taste buds left and will probably love them *[and, believe it or not, you probably will]*.

BONUS: ULCER EXCUSE

I can't eat my vegetables today. I have an ulcer...

... Peas and sweetcorn are not going to help. The one and only cure is Neapolitan Ice Cream.

Book 8: Vegetable Excuses

BONUS: BALANCED DIET EXCUSE

Remember what you said about eating a balanced diet? . . .

. . . Well, these vegetables are rubbish at balancing, so clearly I can't eat them.

BONUS: CARROT CAKE EXCUSE

I have a big announcement . . .

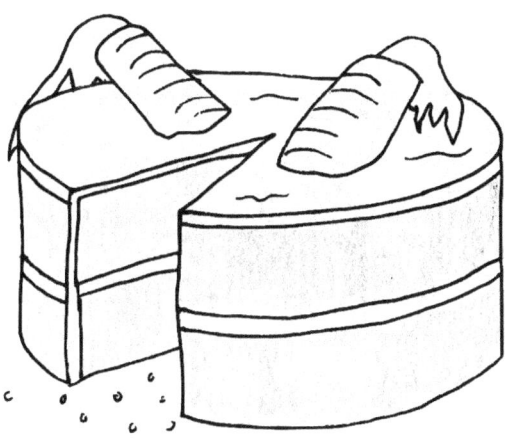

. . . From now on I only eat vegetables that have been baked into cakes. Apparently, carrot cake is very tasty so let's have that for dinner tonight.

Book 8: Vegetable Excuses

BONUS: CRIME SCENE EXCUSE

By the way, the police just called...

... They've informed me that my dinner plate was the scene of a terrible crime. It's been cornered off to preserve the crime scene.

The Excuse Encyclopedia

BONUS: CARNIVORE EXCUSE

I learnt in science today that I am a carnivore...

... That means I can only eat meat. My little sister on the other hand is definitely a herbivore, so she can have all of my vegetables from now on.

Book 8: Vegetable Excuses

BONUS: VEG BEARER EXCUSE

Good news! I have hired a Veg Bearer . . .

. . . This dog will be tasting all my vegetables before I eat them from now on. So far, I haven't been able to eat any of my vegetables as he's very keen to be called a *good boy*.

The Excuse Encyclopedia

BONUS: HEALTHY BIN EXCUSE

Have you noticed our bin is getting a belly?
. . .

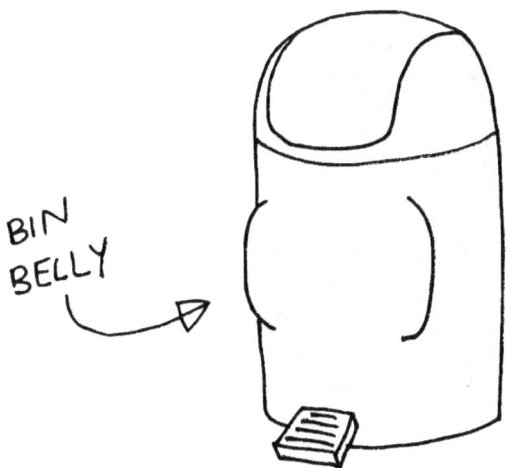

BIN BELLY

. . . I've started a campaign to help our kitchen bin eat healthier. From now on I'm going to throw all of my veggies in the bin and make sure it does twenty sit ups every day.

Book 8: Vegetable Excuses

BONUS: VEG POWER EXCUSE

I can't eat my vegetables tonight . . .

. . . I'm working on new renewable power sources. Pass me your iPhone and I'll charge it up to full power with my veggie power.

BONUS: CANNIBAL EXCUSE

Erm, well, you see... I'm a Brussels sprout...

... Therefore, I can't eat them. One of them could be my long-lost relative.

Book 8: Vegetable Excuses

BONUS: TONGUE-ACHE EXCUSE

You've heard about toothache, right? . . .

. . . Well, I've got a tongueache. Quick, get me every single flavour of ice cream ever invented and the biggest duvet in the world, QUICK!!!

BONUS: RAW VEG EXCUSE

I read a very interesting article online today...

... It said that eating raw vegetables is much healthier than eating cooked vegetables. So, if you eat this raw Brussels sprout than I'll eat my veggies.

Book 8: Vegetable Excuses

BONUS: FUSSY PARASITE EXCUSE

I have a lovely parasite (called Steve) living in my belly . . .

. . . Bad news is that Steve hates vegetables. I'm trying to be a polite host, just like you taught me, so please serve me two slices of Chocolate Cake for dinner tonight. One slice for Steve and one slice for me.

BOOK NINE

Excuses for Not Doing the Washing Up

Book 9: Chore Excuses

1. THE WASHING-UP LIQUID EXCUSE

We've run out of washing-up liquid...

... Why? Because we ran out of shower gel first. Which is more important: clean dishes or clean armpits?

The Excuse Encyclopedia

2. THE DISPOSABLES EXCUSE

Ta-da! I've stockpiled on disposables . . .

. . . Disposable plates. Disposable forks. Disposable knives and cups and spoons and bowls and those little plastic things you find in motorway cafes you use to stir your hot drink. No one will ever have to do the washing up ever again!!!

Book 9: Chore Excuses

3. THE FLAVOUR EXCUSE

You may call them *dirty dishes*, but I call them *flavoured dishes* . . .

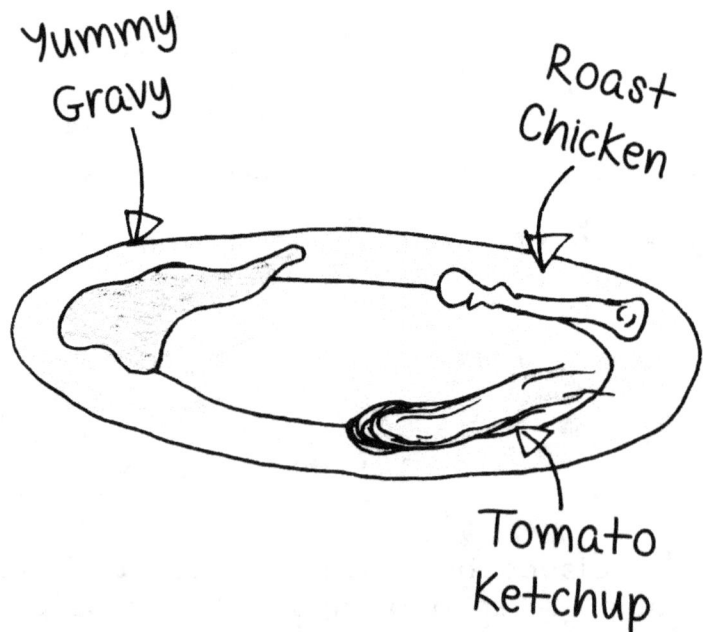

. . . Think about it. You could be eating your dinner with the flavours of yesterday's roast chicken and the aromas of stone-cold homemade gravy with a hint of three-day old tomato ketchup.

The Excuse Encyclopedia

4. THE YELLOW GLOVES EXCUSE

Hang on. You want me to wear these...

hideous yellow washing-up gloves

... Don't you know that yellow is not my colour? Let me know once you've found multicoloured washing-up gloves with galloping unicorns up the arms and rainbow tassels dangling off the sleeves and then I'll do the washing up.

Book 9: Chore Excuses

5. THE DISHWASHER EXCUSE

Don't worry. I've discovered something that will do the washing-up while we all watch the TV...

... It's called a dishwasher. Simply load in your dirty dishes, hit the start button and in one hour the stains are replaced with sparkles. It's arriving tomorrow so let's leave the washing-up and go watch cartoons.

Excuses for Not Emptying the Kitchen Bin

Book 9: Chore Excuses

6. THE DIGGER EXCUSE

Thanks to my digger we now have a bottomless bin...

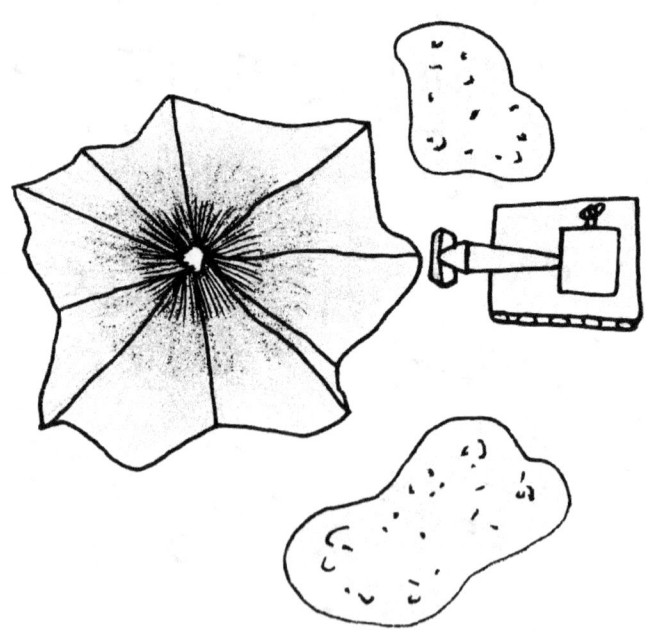

... No need to worry about our garbage anymore. Our rubbish is China's problem now.

The Excuse Encyclopedia

7. THE TRASH MONSTER EXCUSE

I've got a new kitchen bin . . .

. . . He's called Kevin. FYI, he bites.

Book 9: Chore Excuses

8. THE SEA CAPTAIN EXCUSE

Ahoy there, matey . . .

. . . Did you know that in my spare time I am a Pirate Captain. The hull of my Pirate Ship will be made out of empty pop bottles. The cannons will be made out of used toilet rolls. The sails will be made out of lots and lots of empty crisp packets taped together. So let's all get drinking, pooping and munching!

The Excuse Encyclopedia

9. THE BROTHER'S BEDROOM EXCUSE

Hope you don't mind but I've moved the kitchen bin . . .

. . . I know what you're going to say - it's no longer in the kitchen. But I hope you'll agree it's now in a much, much more satisfying location.

Book 9: Chore Excuses

10. THE OVERFLOW EXCUSE

You know the fairy-tale called *Hansel and Gretel* . . .

. . . I'm not going to lure innocent children with a trail of sweets. I'm going to lure an unsuspecting bin man with a trail of rubbish, trap him in the house and tame him to become our very own kitchen bin man.

Excuses for Not Setting the Dinner Table

11. THE CHOPSTICKS EXCUSE

I've thrown away all our cutlery and replaced them with these...

... It's what Asian countries use to eat their dinner. I am yet to master the technique but what I can tell you is that they are very good for picking your nose.

12. THE OPEN WIDE EXCUSE

I've had an idea. I propose that from now on we no longer eat from plates . . .

. . . Instead we take it in turns to sit in front of this target and open our mouths really, really wide. Oh, and I recommend not wearing your favourite t-shirt.

Book 9: Chore Excuses

13. THE WHIRLWIND EXCUSE

I already set the table. Oh no! . . .

. . . It must have been a hurricane, a really really tidy hurricane that who blew all the plates back into the cupboard and all the cutlery back into the drawer.

The Excuse Encyclopedia

14. THE MONOPOLY EXCUSE

I'm changed and ready to be the banker. Oh dear! . . .

. . . I set the table ready to play Monopoly instead of setting the table for dinner. You really should be more specific when you say *'set the table'*.

Book 9: Chore Excuses

15. THE INDIAN EXCUSE

As a family at dinner time, I think we should be more cultured . . .

. . . In India, people use their hands to tear off a strip of naan bread and use it to scoop up their food. So let's ditch the knife and fork and eat like Indians tonight.

Excuses for Not Cleaning the Rabbit Hutch

Book 9: Chore Excuses

16. THE LIFE SWAP EXCUSE

I'm doing a life swap...

... Floppy is going to go to school, do my homework and finish my chores while I sit here on this pile of hay and nibble a carrot.

The Excuse Encyclopedia

17. THE POTTY TRAINING EXCUSE

Has anyone attempted to potty train a rabbit...

... The answer is yes, ME! It's a work in progress but I'm confident it can revolutionise rabbit hutch cleaning for children everywhere.

Book 9: Chore Excuses

18. THE FRAGRANCE EXCUSE

My new rabbit fragrance is going to be the latest perfume fad...

...Floppy is helping me collect and ferment the ingredients: essence of hay, nibbled carrot and concentrated bunny wee wee. It's gonna be huge in New York!

The Excuse Encyclopedia

19. THE MACHINE EXCUSE

I've developed a new state-of-the-art rabbit hutch cleaning machine...

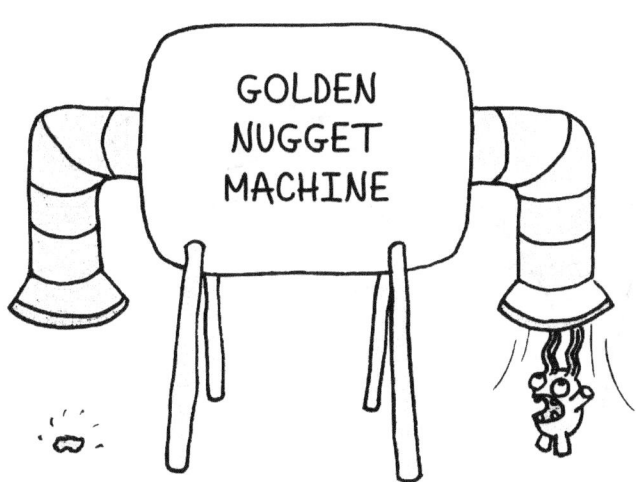

...It's a work in progress but once fully tested I should be able to clean the hutch in five seconds and make us filthy rich.

Book 9: Chore Excuses

20. THE HOUSE RABBIT EXCUSE

I've decided Floppy should be a house rabbit...

... Look at how much he loves the great indoors. Plus, you'll be able to clean up the rabbit poop at the same as hoovering the house.

Excuses for Getting Out of the Weekly Food Shopping Trip

Book 9: Chore Excuses

21. THE STILTS EXCUSE

I need to stay at home and practice stilt walking . . .

. . . That way next week I'll be able to reach anything you want from the top shelf. Curry paste, exotic dried fruits, luxury toilet roll. Nothing will be out of reach for me.

The Excuse Encyclopedia

22. THE SHOPPING PARTNER EXCUSE

If you're looking for a shopping partner, Fido is your best choice . . .

. . . He can fetch on command, he doesn't answer back and if you take him down the sweetie aisle he won't stuff chocolate buttons down his pants.

Book 9: Chore Excuses

23. THE LISTS EXCUSE

Shopping list? Don't worry I brought my own today...

...this list is for Christmas but I've got another for my birthday, another for my next birthday and another for when I become Prime Minster of the United Kingdom.

24. THE TROLLEY EXCUSE

I can't come shopping until I've got my shopping trolley driving licence . . .

. . . I've booked my Theory Test and I am having trolley driving lessons with a qualified instructor. I'm hoping to get my licence and be ready to join you on the weekly food shop in six to twelve months.

Book 9: Chore Excuses

25. THE ACTION MAN EXCUSE

Here's the honest truth. You don't need me to help with the food shop . . .

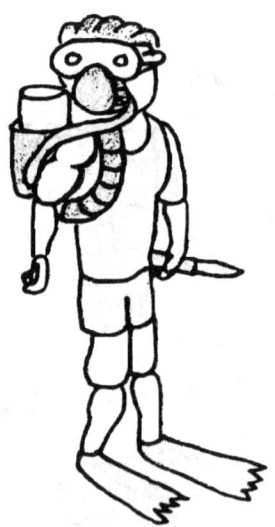

. . . You just want the company. Here, take my action man instead. He'll protect you from soviet spies and listen to your boring gossip about the neighbours.

Excuses for Not Walking the Dog

Book 9: Chore Excuses

26. THE WALKING THE HUMAN EXCUSE

I think I've worked out a way to improve dog walking for everyone...

... Turn it around and the dog walks you. All you need is a wheelie chair, a strong leash and one extremely energetic dog.

27. THE TWO WORDS EXCUSE

I have two words for you. ROBOT DOG! . . .

. . . He doesn't need walking. He doesn't need feeding. He doesn't sleep so he'll always catch burglars. He never poos or whines or pees on the floor when he gets excited.

Book 9: Chore Excuses

28. THE ULTIMATE FETCH EXCUSE

No need to take the dog for a walk anymore...

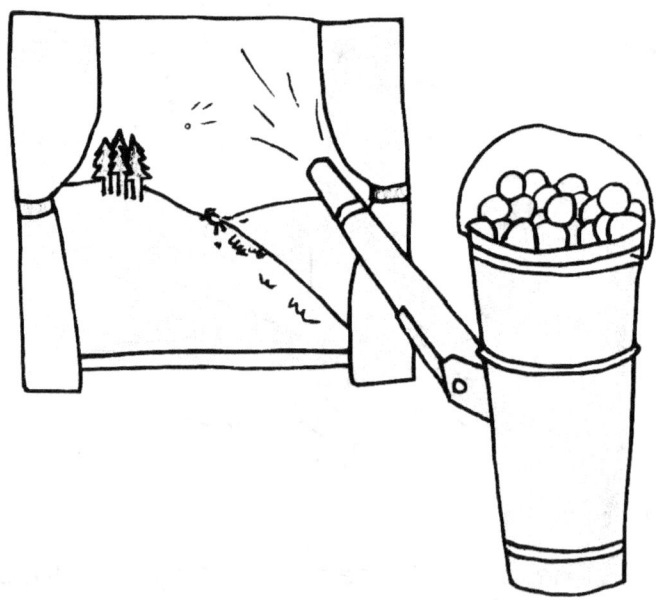

...This cannon will fire tennis balls a distance of 10,000 yards. I've got 100 tennis balls for the dog to go fetch. Fido is going to sleep well tonight!

The Excuse Encyclopedia

29. THE FORGOTTEN EXCUSE

I can't walk the dog . . .

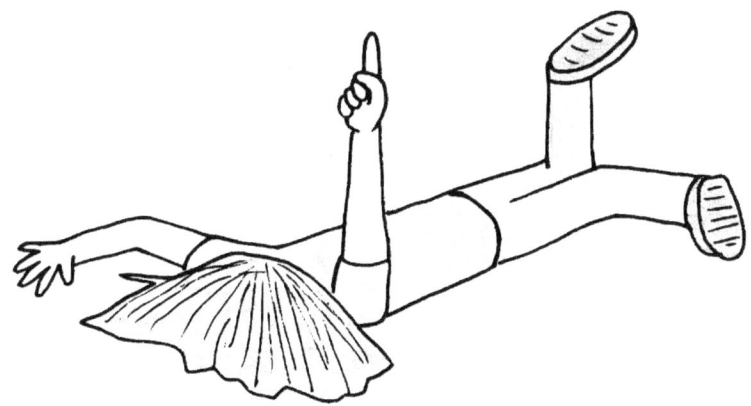

. . . Why? Because I've forgotten how to walk. Got a spare wheelchair?

Book 9: Chore Excuses

30. THE GREAT OUTDOORS EXCUSE

The purpose of the dog walk is for the dog to poo outside . . .

. . . Well, I have the perfect solution. Let's all live outside! Embrace the great outdoors, become one with nature, poop in the bushes. The dog will be on a constant walk!

Excuses for Not Emptying the Cat Litter Tray

Book 9: Chore Excuses

31. THE THERAPY BATH EXCUSE

Did you know that cat poop is very good for your skin . . .

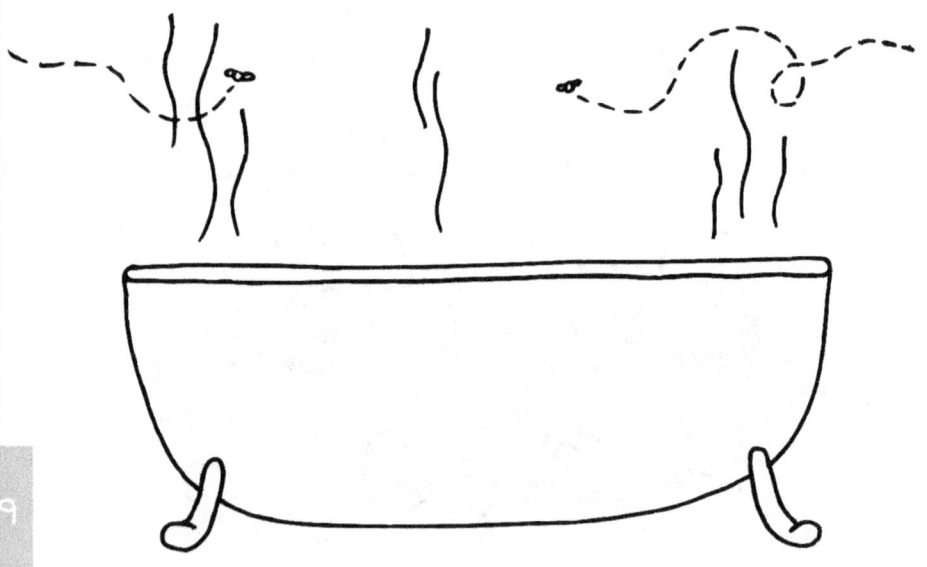

. . . That's why I've moved the Litter Tray to the bath tub so you can have a De-Wrinkling Cat Poop Therapy Bath. You'll need to wait a couple of months before there is enough to fully submerge your whole body.

The Excuse Encyclopedia

32. THE NEIGHBOURS EXCUSE

Solved it! The cat can climb, right? . . .

. . . Good, because I've decided to move the litter tray. Now that it is on top of the neighbour's garage the litter tray is their problem now.

Book 9: Chore Excuses

33. THE OPEN WINDOW EXCUSE

Nobody remembers to clean the litter tray...

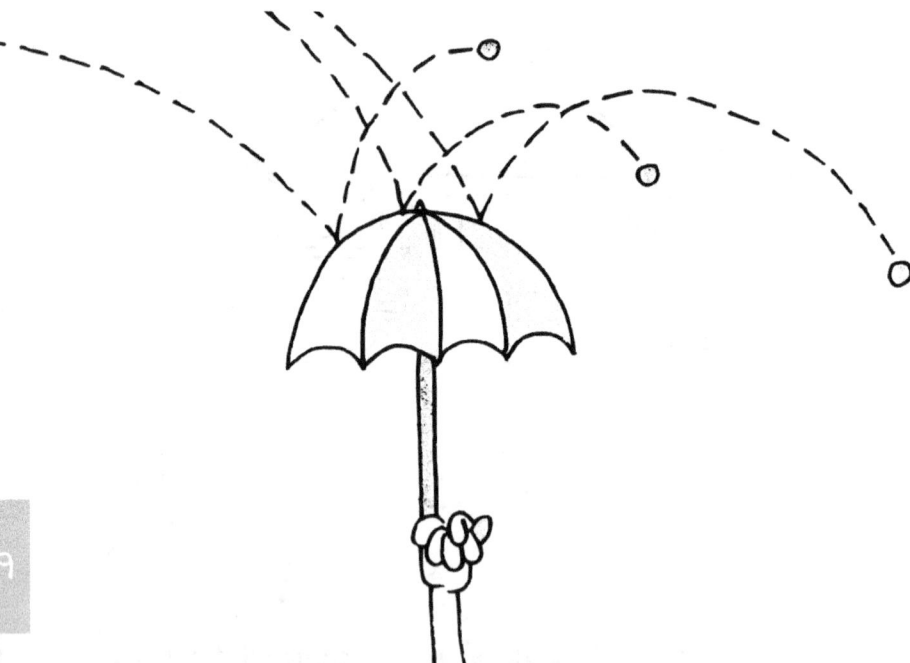

...So I've taken it upon myself to train Felix to poop out the window. From now on everyone will need to remember to use this umbrella whenever you leave or enter the house.

The Excuse Encyclopedia

34. THE CAT NAPPY EXCUSE

Why has no-one thought of this before? .
. .

. . . I call it the Cat Nappy. Simply replace every night and no one will have to empty the Litter Tray ever again.

Book 9: Chore Excuses

35. THE AGREEMENT EXCUSE

The cat and I have come to a mutual arrangement...

...I will ensure that her chin is scratched for 30 minutes a day and she'll always poop in the neighbour's garden. I hope you agree that this is a pretty good deal.

Excuses for Not Doing the Drying Up

Book 9: Chore Excuses

36. THE TEA TOWEL EXCUSE

Ah, we've run out of tea towels . . .

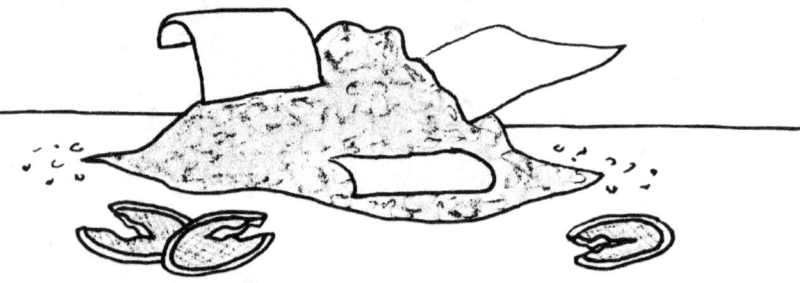

. . . So, I tried to make some new ones from scratch. Could you pop to the shops and buy tea bags and paper towels. My first attempts were unsuccessful but I'm close to finding the perfect blend.

The Excuse Encyclopedia

37. THE WET EXCUSE

How can I do the drying up? . . .

. . . I'm soaking wet. I'll never be able to make anything dry ever again! On the other hand, I'll be very helpful when the plants need watering or the dog bowl needs filling.

Book 9: Chore Excuses

38. THE EMPLOYEE EXCUSE

I've hired some help to do the drying up. . .

. . . So far Nelly is yet to perfect the optimum blowing strength to dry the washing up. You are going to need to buy new plates, bowls, glasses, tea cups, side plates, coffee mugs, and those tiny little cups you drink espresso from.

39. THE WASHING LINE EXCUSE

I've had an epiphany . . .

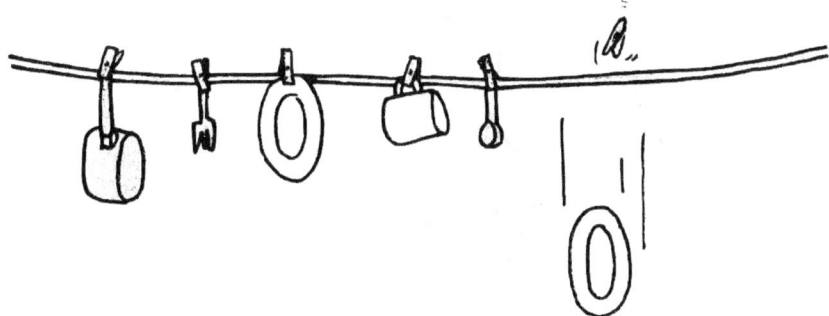

. . . We dry our clothes on the washing line, so maybe we should also dry the washing up here too. We can put our feet up and eat an ice cream while the sun does all the hard work for us.

Book 9: Chore Excuses

40. THE UNDER THE SEA EXCUSE

Let's live under the sea . . .

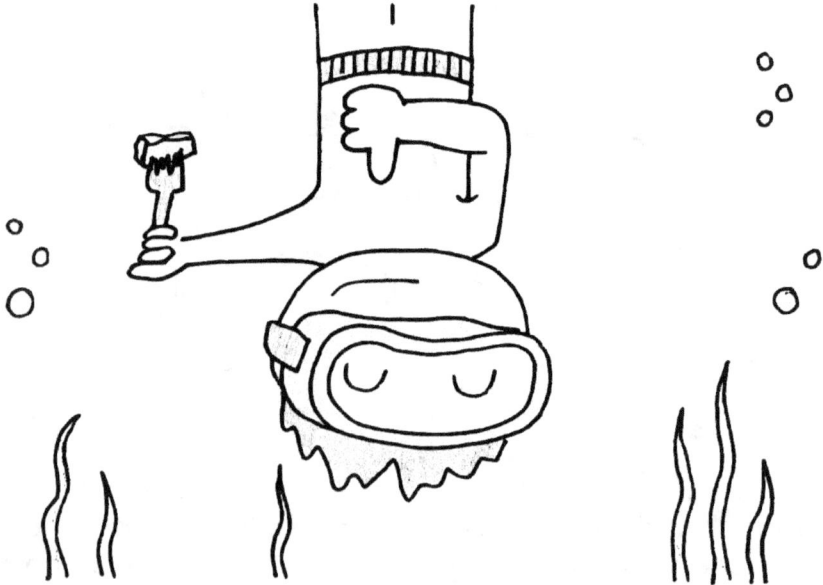

. . . No one would ever have to do the drying up ever again. Plus, I could make friends with a singing crab and go on an adventure to find a lost fish.

Excuses for Not Mowing the Lawn

Book 9: Chore Excuses

41. THE JUNGLE EXCUSE

You said no to a pet monkey because we don't have a big enough house...

...So I'm cultivating a jungle habitat in the garden. I'm halfway there to a full jungle enclosure so do not bring any sharp objects near the foliage.

The Excuse Encyclopedia

42. THE PROTECTED HABITAT EXCUSE

STOP! My name is Basil Von Licktonshoe and I am a Wildlife Preservation Officer...

... I have an official document to declare your garden as a Protected Habitat for Rare and Endangered Weeds. Never ask your child to mow the lawn or you'll be fined £100,000 and will be banned from all garden centres for life.

Book 9: Chore Excuses

43. THE HAIRDRESSER EXCUSE

When I grow up I want to be a Hairdresser . . .

. . . Which means it's against my occupation to 'mow'. Instead I can 'snip', 'perm' or 'highlight' the lawn for a small fee while gossiping about B-List Celebrities.

44. THE WEATHER EXCUSE

I'd love to mow the lawn but first let's check the Weather Forecast . . .

THURS	FRI	SAT	SUN
rain	thunderstorm	wind	sun

. . . Oh dear. Can't do it in the rain as it's bad for the grass. Can't do it in a thunder storm as I could get struck by lightning. Can't do it in strong winds as it will ruin my hair do. Can't do it in the sunshine as I'll be in the paddling pool drinking ice cold lemonade.

45. THE BOWING EXCUSE

Are you sure you said 'mow the lawn' . . .

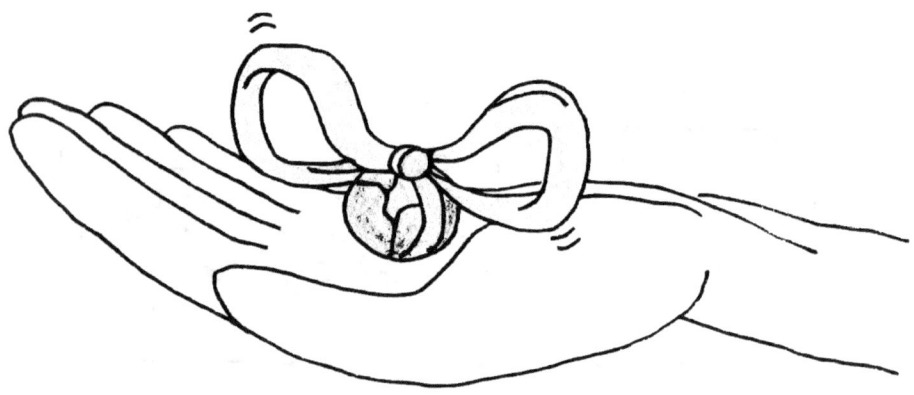

. . . I thought you said 'bow the corn'. Thought that was a strange request, but on the bright side I am now an expert at bowing small vegetables.

Excuses for Not Doing the Hoovering

Book 9: Chore Excuses

46. THE SPIDER KINGDOM EXCUSE

I can't do the hoovering . . .

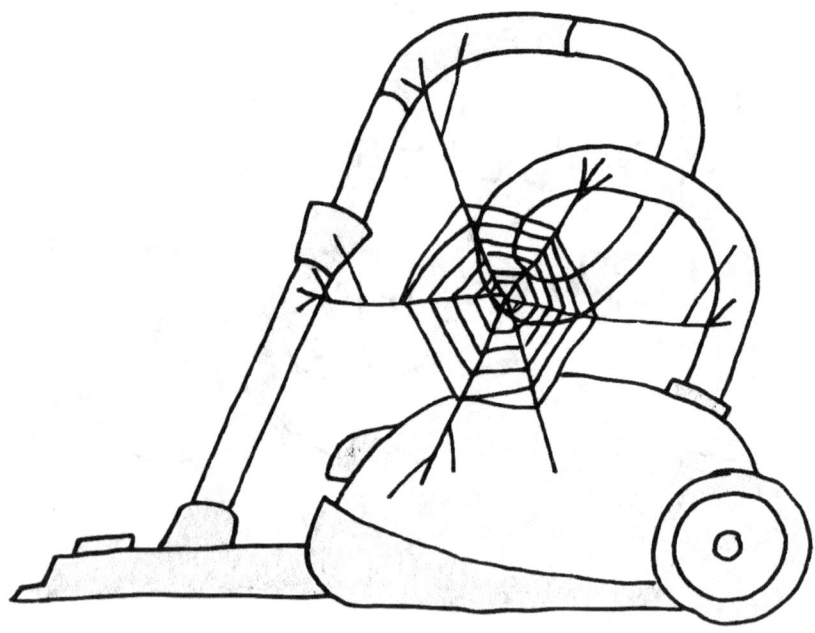

. . . Last week I hoovered up a massive spider. I fear that it has now made the vacuum it's Spider Kingdom, over which it holds full sovereignty.

47. THE ONE HOUR EXCUSE

Sorry I can't hoover until one hour after eating . . .

. . . That's right, it's very similar to swimming. The same applies to Maths homework and answering the question "How was your day?"

Book 9: Chore Excuses

48. THE DEFLECTION EXCUSE

I want to do the hoovering, but I can't until my older sister has cleared the floor . . .

. . . And before she can clear the floor my older brother needs to do the dusting. And before he can do the dusting Dad needs to take us all out for an ice cream.

49. THE OLYMPIAN EXCUSE

Hoovering the stairs would disrupt my strict training regime . . .

. . . I will be entering the next Winter Olympics as a ski jumper and so I need the stairs to be as dusty as possible to simulate snow. I expect it will take at least 6 months of no hoovering to get to optimum skiing practice levels.

Book 9: Chore Excuses

BONUS: IRONING EXCUSE

Sorry, I can't do the ironing . . .

. . . You see, I don't live in the Iron Age. I live in the Digital Age.

BONUS: 'RESET' THE TABLE EXCUSE

Oh, I seem to have misheard you . . .

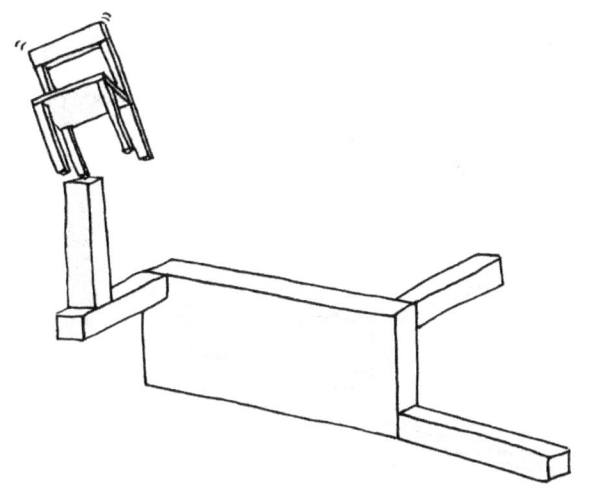

. . . I have 'reset' the table instead of 'set' the table. So our dining room table is now a piece of modern art.

Book 9: Chore Excuses

BONUS: SAWDUST EVERYWHERE EXCUSE

I've found the perfect cleaning solution.

... Fill the entire house with sawdust. If you can't find the toilet, it doesn't matter. You can go anywhere you like, just like a rabbit.

The Excuse Encyclopedia

BONUS: ONE CONDITION EXCUSE

I'll happily join you on the weekly food shop . . .

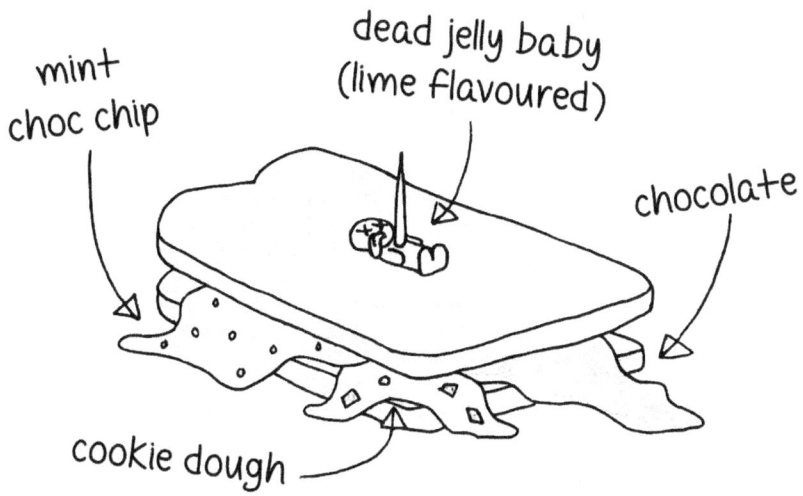

. . . but I have one condition. We have Ice Cream Sandwiches for dinner tonight.

Book 9: Chore Excuses

BONUS: DOG PEN EXCUSE

No need to take the dog for a walk today . . .

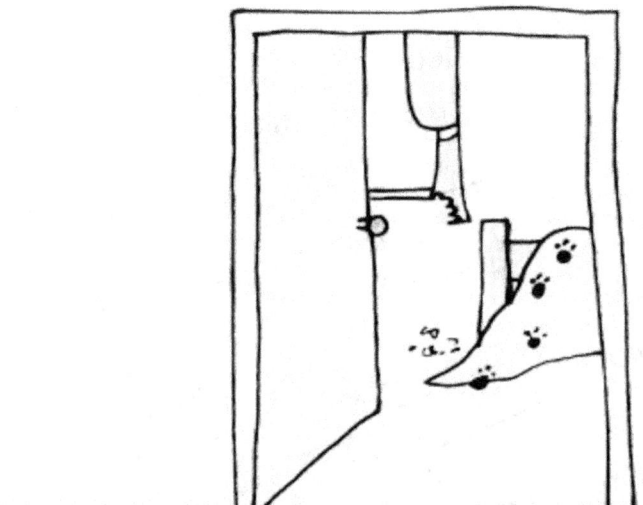

. . . he's in the new dog pen I've made. I admit that it didn't have to be in your bedroom, but you do have the most space and the nicest views.

BONUS: EVIL CAT EXCUSE

I think our cat is evil . . .

. . . He always looks like he is plotting something. Don't clean the litter tray! I'll go call the Bomb Squad just to be on the safe side.

Book 9: Chore Excuses

BONUS: MISSING EARRING EXCUSE

WAIT! Mum says I shouldn't mow the lawn . . .

. . . She lost her earring when she was watering the plants this morning. You take the magnifying glass and I'll take the binoculars.

The Excuse Encyclopedia

BONUS: FAIRY EXCUSE

No, I have not washed the dishes . . .

. . . but I have been dashing wishes. That's right, I'm a Fairy Wish Dasher.

Book 9: Chore Excuses

BONUS: MOUSE ESCAPE EXCUSE

When I went to pick up my dirty laundry I discovered this . . .

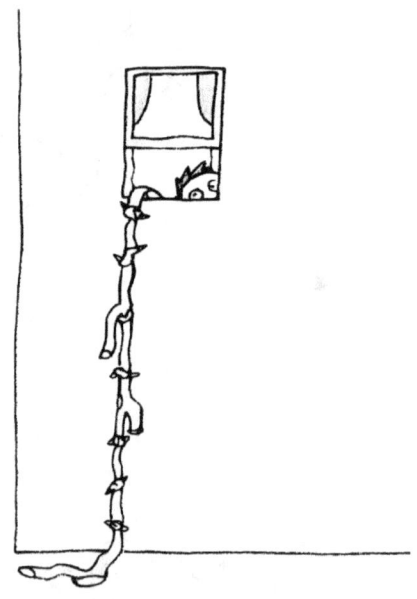

. . . As you can see, all my dirty laundry has been tied together and is hanging out of my bedroom. My pet mouse, Nibbles, has made a run for it.

BONUS: ECO-WARRIOR ESCAPE EXCUSE

I believe that cleaning is an act of violence against nature...

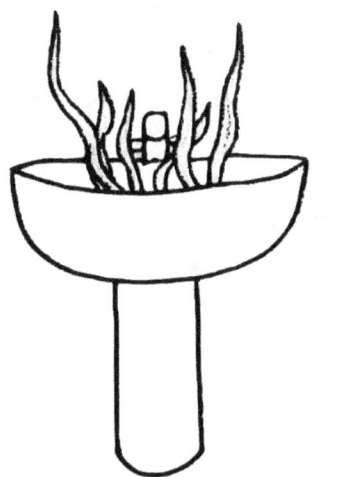

...Instead of attacking the natural world and our co-inhabitants, we should learn to live together in harmony. Join me and never clean anything ever again.

Book 9: Chore Excuses

BONUS: DIZZY EXCUSE

I did start my chores . . .

. . . but then I began to feel dizzy. Can you see the stars and bird and lizard with a moustache flying around my head? Maybe I should go and sit down.

The Excuse Encyclopedia

BONUS: BIG DISCOVERY EXCUSE

WAIT! I can't mop the kitchen floor . . .

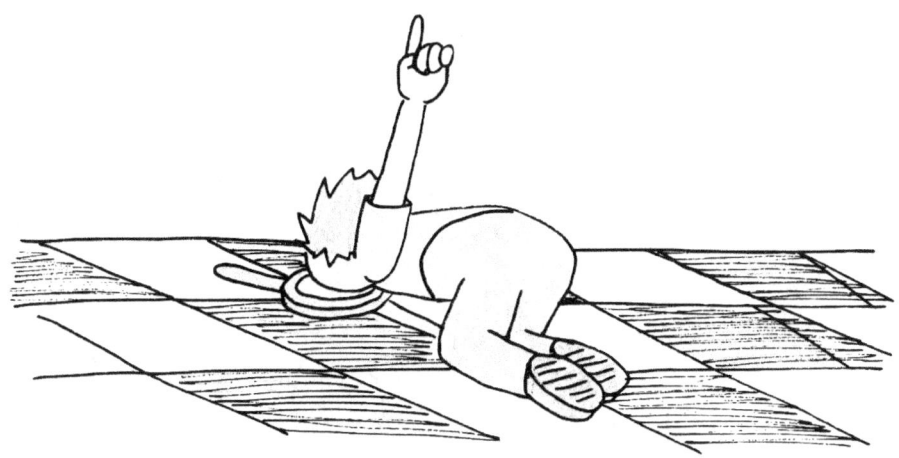

. . . I've made an important scientific discovery. I am not sure what it is yet but give me two to three weeks and I might win the Nobel Prize.

Book 9: Chore Excuses

BONUS: SEAT WARMER EXCUSE

But I am doing my chores? . . .

. . . I am currently warming this seat ready for when mum comes home from work. I think that it is the most important task on my chores list.

The Excuse Encyclopedia

BONUS: ULTRA VEGAN EXCUSE

Nope. I can't do my chores. Why? Because I am now an Ultra Vegan...

...I believe that humans should not kill any living thing, including bacteria with all of those nasty cleaning products. From now on I will be staying inside this circle so I don't accidentally squish any little innocent microbes.

Book 9: Chore Excuses

BONUS: ONLINE CHORES EXCUSE

I can't do my chores now because I am doing my online chores . . .

. . . On my tablet, Sandy my online SIM, is currently cleaning the bathroom and then she needs to mow the lawn wash the car and cook the dinner. So, as you can see, I am far too busy.

BONUS: ICE SKATING EXCUSE

Maybe I shouldn't mop the floor today?..

...It's the coldest day of the year today, so if I mop the floor the water could turn the kitchen into an ice skating rink.

Book 9: Chore Excuses

BONUS: DREAM IDEAS EXCUSE

I know I'm late, but I can make up for it..

(bacteria-Z-oo)
ZZZ
(snee-Z-e train)
ZZZZZZZ
(Z-ebra socks)
ZZZ

... Thanks to the extra sleep I got this morning I had more time to dream up some exciting new business ideas. *[Insert quirky, funny business ideas here to make all your class mates laugh].* So, what do you think, Miss? Would you like to invest in one of my new businesses?

The Excuse Encyclopedia

BONUS: ARMY OF ANTS EXCUSE

Bad news. The dustpan and brush are broken...

... So, I've come up with an inventive solution to clean the kitchen floor. This is my army of ants. I'm going to shout orders at them while eating this sandwich.

Book 9: Chore Excuses

BONUS: NO HANDS EXCUSE

In order to do the washing up you need to have hands . . .

. . . But, due to accidentally chopping off my hands in a tragic nail clipping accident, I no longer have any hands.

BOOK TEN

Excuses for Dodging the Dreaded Christmas Day Walk

Book 10: Christmas Excuses

1. THE INDOOR WALK EXCUSE

Christmas dinner was delicious. Thank you, but you'll have to go on without me...

... I'm now so round I've lost the use of my legs. You all go on the Christmas walk and I'll stay at home and burn off the Christmas Dinner calories by rolling around the living room to 'Rockin' Around the Christmas Tree'.

2. THE SECURITY EXCUSE

Go on a walk? Now? Fine, but someone has to stand guard...

... All these lovely presents need to be protected against the Grinch, common thieves, master criminals, the Borrowers, and let's not forget Kevin. You know, the spotty kid next door who has sticky fingers and collects shiny things.

Book 10: Christmas Excuses

3. THE REPLACEMENT ANGEL EXCUSE

Oh no! Where did the angel on top of the Christmas Tree go? . . .

. . . It's a holiday disaster. Christmas is ruined. Unless, I don't go on the Christmas walk, dress like an angel, and perch on top of the tree with my trademark angelic smile.

4. THE GHOST EXCUSE

I can't go on the walk because I'm expecting an important visitor...

... Who? The ghost of Christmas Future. Apparently being a Scrooge, saying 'bah humbug', and not getting into the Christmas spirit will get you haunted. So if you want a better present next year you should leave me behind so that I can become a better person.

5. THE EMERGENCY CALL EXCUSE

Bad news. Just got off the phone with the Temp Agency . . .

. . . Father Christmas needs emergency workers to finish all his deliveries. They're offering double pay for working Christmas Day. It was an offer too good to refuse. My delivery rounds are Hungary, then Switzerland and finishing with Norway. Save me a mince pie.

Excuses for Forgetting Someone's Christmas Present

Book 10: Christmas Excuses

6. THE 'ME' EXCUSE

Ah. Your Christmas present . . . Your present is . . . erm . . .

. . . Me! I know, best Christmas present EVER. Here are some important instructions to keep your new present healthy and happy. Bedtime is 23:00, it needs a chocolate coin every hour, and if it eats a vegetable it'll turn into a little monster.

7. THE POSTMAN EXCUSE

Where's your present? I sent it in the post . . .

. . . Come to think of it the parcel should have arrived by now. If your postman is wearing stripy gloves with a matching scarf and bobble hat then make sure you report them for postal theft.

Book 10: Christmas Excuses

8. THE ENLIGHTENMENT EXCUSE

Sit down, cross your legs and close your eyes . . .

. . . Meditate like this for three years and you'll gain the best present this life can possibly offer – *inner peace.* You can thank me in three years' time. Now then, if you need me, I'll be seeking inner awesomeness by completing my new video game I got for Christmas.

9. THE PERFECTION EXCUSE

You know how I'm the perfect child? . . .

. . . Well, my Christmas present to you is one whole week of intensive training. I'll teach you how to be perfect just like me.

10. THE SPIRIT PET EXCUSE

I found the perfect present for you . . .

. . . I discovered your spirit animal. It's this toad. So, my Christmas present to you is your soul pet. He lives at the bottom of the garden, enjoys long walks on the beach and answers to Kevin.

Excuses for Leaving your Brussels Sprouts

CHRISTMAS EXCUSES

10

11. THE DOGS DINNER EXCUSE

Why have I left my Brussels sprouts? . . .

. . . Because these Brussels sprouts are my Christmas present to the dog. I can't wait to give them to him. He's gonna love 'em!

12. THE BELGIAN HERITAGE EXCUSE

Did you know that I'm half Belgian . . .

. . . In my homeland we never eat Brussels sprouts on Christmas Day. Never. It is considered an offence to eat anything green at all. We only eat Belgian chocolate.

Book 10: Christmas Excuses

13. THE REINDEER SNACKS EXCUSE

You know how we leave carrots out on Christmas Eve for the reindeer . . .

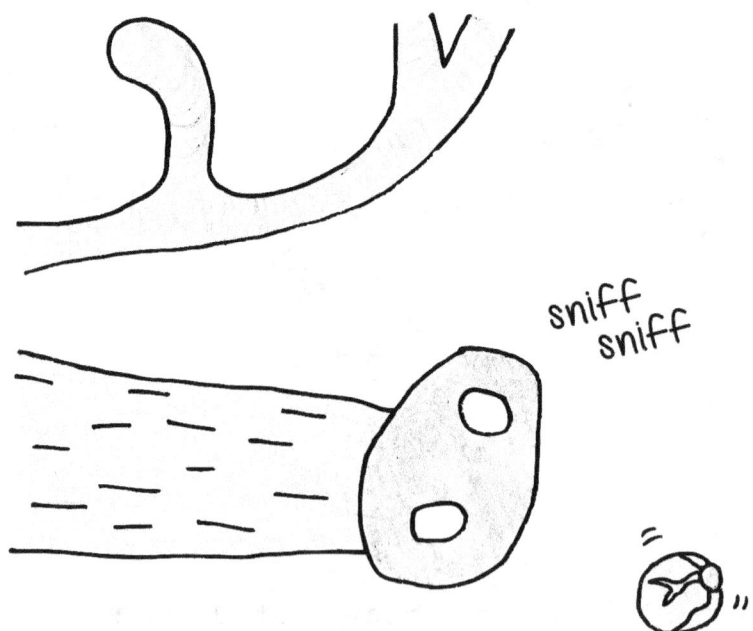

. . . Well, someone told me that we also have to leave Brussels sprouts outside for the return journey. Apparently, the extra gas helps the reindeer get home to the north pole in time for supper.

The Excuse Encyclopedia

14. THE VEGAN BAUBLES EXCUSE

I have had a wonderful business idea . . .

. . . Vegan-Friendly Baubles. They're Brussels sprouts, which means they're both Christmassy and edible (but definitely not suitable for children).

15. THE BANNED EXCUSE

The Queen of England has banned Brussels sprouts! . . .

. . . She announced it in her Christmas Speech while you were on the loo. I'm afraid that it would be an act of high treason against the royal crown of the British Monarchy to eat them now.

Book 10: Christmas Excuses

16. THE ALARM EXCUSE

Who set the alarm clock for 5am?!? . . .

. . . Well it wasn't me, so it must have been Rudolf. You know, the red-nosed reindeer. He's such a prankster. So, now that everyone is up and wide awake, which presents are for me?

17. THE CLOCKS EXCUSE

Look, it's 7am!! . . .

. . . If you don't believe me then go ahead and check every single clock in the house. Admittedly the oven clock was the hardest to change but definitely worth it.

Book 10: Christmas Excuses

18. THE BREAKFAST EXCUSE

I couldn't sleep because I was really, really hungry...

... So, I decided to make a Christmas breakfast for everyone. I didn't know what you'd like to eat so I made quite a lot. Eat up before it gets cold.

19. THE NIGHTMARE EXCUSE

I can't sleep. I had a terrible nightmare. . .

. . . I dreamt that I'm going to sleep in past 7am. Gulp! Then I wake up shivering in a pool of cold sweat terrified that I'm going to sleep in on Christmas Day.

Book 10: Christmas Excuses

20. THE WEATHER UPDATE EXCUSE

Good morning and welcome to your personal early morning weather update...

THURS	FRI	SAT	SUN
🌧	⛈	💨	☀️

...You can expect a wonderful start to the day, full of smiles and laughter and light showers of wrapping paper. Over lunchtime the temperature is set to shoot up (for the turkey) followed by naps on the sofa. When we reach the evening a cloud of competitiveness will descend with potential for outbreaks of thunder and lightning (depending on who wins the family board game).

Christmas Excuses

Excuses for Having Chocolate for Breakfast

21. THE CHOCOLATE ON TOAST EXCUSE

I normally have chocolate spread on toast for breakfast...

... But, seeing as it is Christmas Day, I've decided to skip the spread and just have chocolate on toast. How long do you think I should put it in the microwave for so that it goes lovely and melty?

22. THE REPLACEMENT CUTLERY EXCUSE

For breakfast I'm going to have a simple bowl of cereal . . .

Chocolate

. . . in a bowl made of chocolate. And I'll eat it with a spoon made of chocolate. Oh, and I'll use chocolate milk and drink the dregs at the bottom of the bowl with a chocolate straw.

Book 10: Christmas Excuses

23. THE HEATWAVE EXCUSE

There's going to be a Christmas heatwave. Quickly, eat all the chocolate before it melts . . .

. . . Oh, hang on. I was looking at the weather forecast for Australia by accident. Whoops.

24. THE HOT CHOCOLATE EXCUSE

Good morning and Happy Christmas. I've made you a lovely big mug of hot chocolate . . .

. . . What would I like for breakfast? I'd like a lovely big mug of cold chocolate please.

Book 10: Christmas Excuses

25. THE FOUNTAIN EXCUSE

Ta-da. Here is your wonderful Christmas present . . .

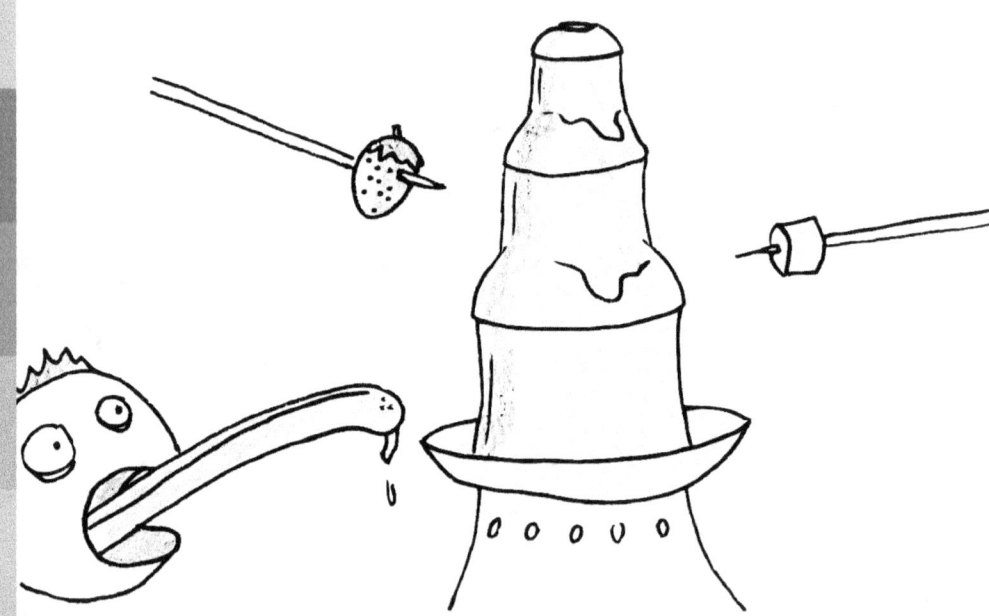

. . . The Choco-Fountain 5000. I thought you'd want to give this baby a go straight away so I set it up ready for Christmas morning breakfast.

Ways to Capture Father Christmas

CHRISTMAS EXCUSES

Book 10: Christmas Excuses

26. THE SLEEPING POWDER EXCUSE

I made bedtime drinks . . .

an extra STRENGTH cup of COFFEE

a lovely glass of UNTAMPERED MILK

. . . The coffee is for me and the milk is for Father Christmas. Did I slip sleeping powder into his milk so he'd fall asleep and leaving his magical sleigh full of presents unguarded? That's a terrible accusation to make. Now if you'll excuse me, I have a long night ahead.

27. THE SURPRISE ATTACK EXCUSE

So, here's the plan . . .

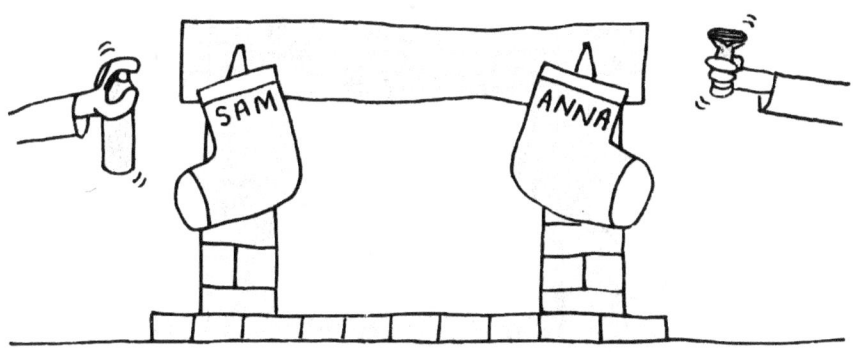

. . . Once Father Christmas falls down the chimney, I'll cover him in shaving cream and you'll quickly shave his beard off. Then we'll post his picture on the internet and wait for his mum to identify him and tell him off for being out so late.

Book 10: Christmas Excuses

28. THE TRAP EXCUSE

How do you catch an old man who's been on his feet all day and all night? . . .

. . . Easy. Leave a pair of slippers next to a comfy chair with an episode of Countdown on the TV. It's almost too easy!

29. THE PLANE TICKET EXCUSE

Right then, I'm off...

... My plane to Australia awaits. But don't worry, I won't miss Christmas. I'll spend Christmas Day in the down-under and quickly take a return plane home. That way I'll have two attempts to snap a photo of Father Christmas.

30. THE STRAY ELF EXCUSE

Shh. I'm not Matt, I'm Kevin the lost workshop Elf . . .

. . . My plan is to hitch a lift with Father Christmas to his secret lair in Lapland. Then I'll sneak into his bedroom, find his passport, and bring it back to prove he really does exist and reveal his real name to the world.

Excuses for Not Doing the Christmas Washing Up

CHRISTMAS EXCUSES

10

31. THE LEFTOVERS EXCUSE

Don't clear away the plates just yet . . .

. . . Christmas Dinner isn't finished. There is so much food left over I made it into a mountain. It may take all week to eat but we can't let anything go to waste.

32. THE NEW TECHNIQUE EXCUSE

Let's test my new washing up technique.

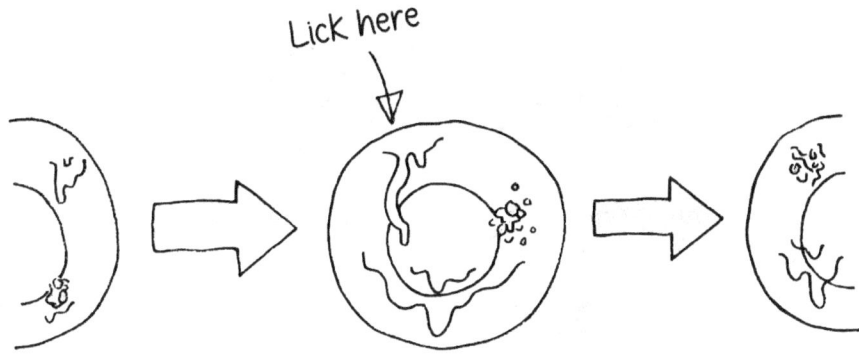

. . . Simply pass your empty plate to the left, lick it, then pass it on to the right. If my calculations are correct then I estimate that once the plates have gone around the table three to four times they will be spotless.

Book 10: Christmas Excuses

33. THE CAROLLING INSTRUCTIONS EXCUSE

I've decided to re-enact my favourite Christmas Carols...

... So, I've asked granddad to have a nap for *God Rest Ye Merry Gentlemen,* the cat is wearing a grey pillowcase for *Little Donkey,* grandma is listening out for bikes and text notifications for *I Heard the Bells on Christmas Day* and I'm attempting to balance this delicious American snack on this tower of washing up for *Ding Dong Merrily on High.*

34. THE UNCLE CHRISTMAS EXCUSE

Last night we left cookies, milk and carrots for Father Christmas and his reindeer . . .

. . . Well, on Christmas Day night we have to leave our dirty dishes. Who for? For Uncle Christmas, of course (he was getting jealous of his older brother getting all the limelight).

Book 10: Christmas Excuses

35. THE TOAST EXCUSE

Before we do the washing up I'd like to give a toast...

... So, put your orders in. You can have peanut butter, chocolate spread or both.

Excuses for Not Taking Down the Tree

CHRISTMAS EXCUSES

Book 10: Christmas Excuses

36. THE NEW SONG EXCUSE

Good news. I've been commissioned by Christmas to write a new Christmas Song...

... I call it 365 Days of Christmas. It's like 12 Days of Christmas but you can sing it every day of the year and celebrate Christmas all year round!

The Excuse Encyclopedia

37. THE ALL-YEAR EXCUSE

Don't put the tree down!!! . . .

. . . I've made *tree decorations* for the rest of the year. Here's the New Year Decorations and we've got Pancake Day, Easter, Summer Holidays, and Hallowe'en decorations to look forward to.

Book 10: Christmas Excuses

38. THE BOXING DAY LUNCH EXCUSE

Time to take down the tree...

... Brian the beaver is working on it now. It will probably take him all week to finish his lunch, after all, he is only a little critter.

39. THE PHOTO TREE EXCUSE

No need to take down the Christmas Tree as I've transformed it in to a Picture Tree . . .

. . . No more edible baubles or silly tinsel in sight. Instead you can hang photos from the branches and my delightful art work.

Book 10: Christmas Excuses

40. THE BIRDS NEST EXCUSE

I was taking down the Christmas tree when I found a nest . . .

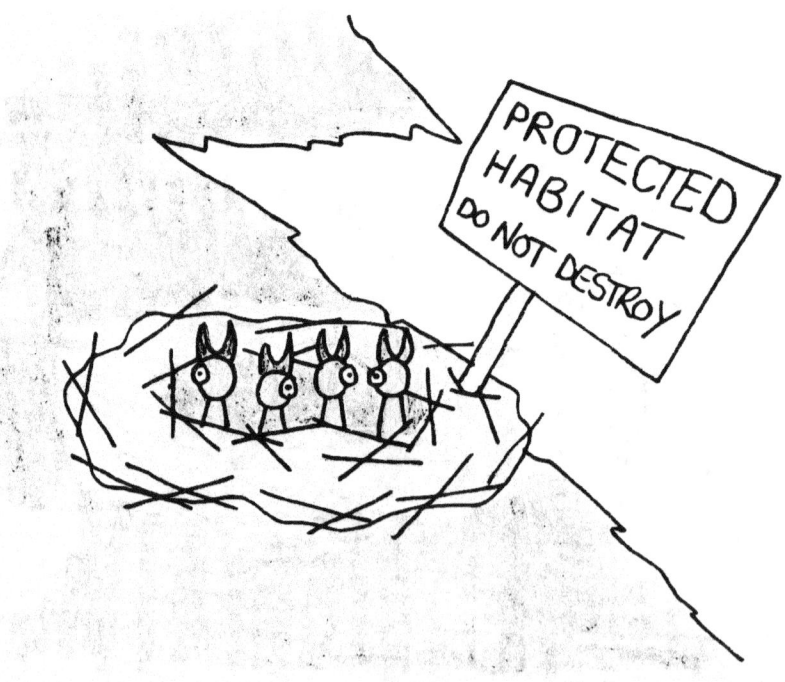

. . . A bird's nest. Look. Four little chicks nesting in our Christmas tree. Except this is no longer our Christmas tree, because it has now become their home. And we can't destroy their home, it's Christmas.

Excuses for Not Going to the Christmas Church Service

Book 10: Christmas Excuses

41. THE WRONG DATE EXCUSE

I want to go to Church on Jesus' real birthday...

... According to theologians we've all got it wrong. His birthday is 11th September and not 25th December. So, I'll be going to Church on 11th September to celebrate the birth of Jesus, I do hope there will be cake.

The Excuse Encyclopedia

42. THE DAY OFF EXCUSE

Did you miss the memo? Jesus has given everyone the day off . . .

. . . Humanity has been told to stay at home in their pyjamas and watch Christmas movies all day. He really is a nice guy.

Book 10: Christmas Excuses

43. THE SNOWED IN EXCUSE

Looked outside. It's snowing! . . .

. . . We shouldn't go to church in a blizzard. It would be a very dangerous journey. We should ask ourselves, what would Jesus do? Personally, I think he'd go sledging.

44. THE FANCY DRESS EXCUSE

Is the Christmas Day Church service fancy dress? . . .

. . . If not then it should be. Can I go as Baby Jesus?

Book 10: Christmas Excuses

45. THE INVITATION EXCUSE

Sorry, I can't go to church today...

... I found this at the bottom of my stocking. It's from Father Christmas. He has invited me to his church's Christmas Day service in Lapland. I'd better get going or I'll miss the first carol.

Excuses for Staying Up Really, Really Late

46. THE LATE NIGHT SPEECH EXCUSE

We've all watched the Queen's Christmas Speech, it was a good one this year...

... This year she will also be doing a Late-Night Christmas Speech after the Royal Family's Christmas Bash. I hear it's wild, she'll probably be wearing a paper hat and slurring her words. Can I stay up to watch it?

47. THE BOARD GAMES EXCUSE

Let's play a board game before bed...

... Can Grandpa play? He always takes ages to take his turn. Which one takes longer? Scrabble, Monopoly or Trivial Pursuit?

Book 10: Christmas Excuses

48. THE ANOTHER ONE EXCUSE

Go on, have another glass of mulled wine . . .

. . . And then have another Baileys followed by a cheeky sherry. When you've fallen asleep in front of the telly I promise I'll go to bed on time and sleep like an angel.

49. THE PLEASE EXCUSE

But, but, but . . .

Mum... could I have a Cookie........please?!

. . . It's the most special day of the whole year! . . . I want the opportunity to enjoy as much of Christmas Day as possible which means staying up until 23.59pm. To the very last minute. If I go to bed now I'll have to wait another 365 days. Please let me stay up late tonight.

Book 10: Christmas Excuses

BONUS: BIG PRESENT EXCUSE

So, I know that I've been a disappointment this year...

... but when Christmas Day arrives and I present you with this present you'll be glad that you put up with all my excuses.

The Excuse Encyclopedia

BONUS: SURGERY EXCUSE

Sorry I'm late, Miss . . .

. . . I've been scheduled for emergency surgery to remove the Christmas Music that is stuck in my head. It's a risky procedure and it'll take four weeks to recover but I think you'll agree it'll all be worth it.

Book 10: Christmas Excuses

BONUS: CHRISTMAS EVE X 35 EXCUSE

Happy Christmas eve, eve, eve, eve, eve, eve, eve, eve, eve, eve, eve, eve, eve, eve, eve, eve, eve, eve, eve, eve, eve, eve, eve, eve, eve, eve, eve, eve, eve, eve, eve, eve, eve, eve, eve . . .

. . . What? No, there isn't thirty-five girls called Eve standing behind you. I just thought you might want to start celebrating Christmas early this year? I am available for mince pie and advent calendar tasting if needed.

The Excuse Encyclopedia

BONUS: MARIAH CAREY EXCUSE

I had to go tell the singer, Mariah Carey something . . .

. . . I had to go all the way to Hollywood to tell that weirdo she can't have me for Christmas. I'm just a kid, that would be illegal and far beyond Father Christmas' abilities. I'm pretty sure he is not involved in human trafficking. I suggest you should go to Hollywood and do the same.

Book 10: Christmas Excuses

BONUS: BREAKING NEWS EXCUSE

BREAKING NEWS! . . .

. . . You can give me my present today. The worlds top Theologians now officially agreed that Jesus was actually born on *[insert date of your choosing here]*. Come on, we both know you've bought my Christmas presents early and they are at the back of your wardrobe.

The Excuse Encyclopedia

BONUS: CHRISTMAS LIGHT EXCUSE

I'll be able to join you on the Christmas walk . . .

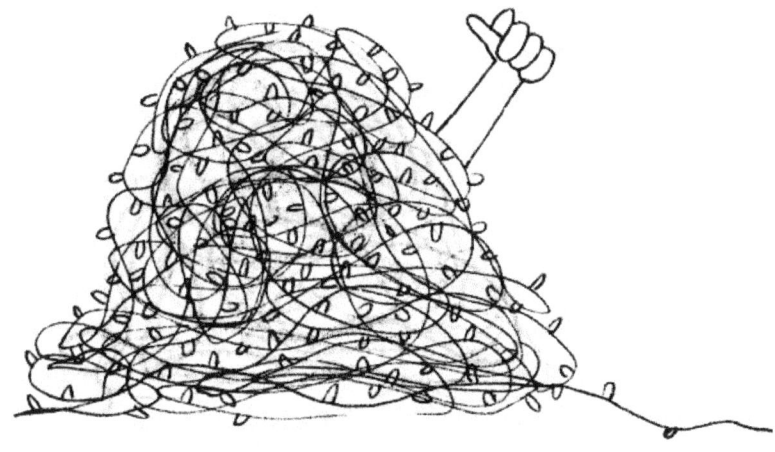

. . . just as soon as I've untangled these Christmas Tree Lights. I estimate I'll be with you no sooner than 5th January.

Book 10: Christmas Excuses

BONUS: LAST MINUTE PRESENT EXCUSE

This year I struggled to find you a Christmas present...

... but then last night I listened to a famous Christmas song and found some inspiration. You've got a pear tree in your garden, haven't you?

BONUS: MISTLETOE POISONING EXCUSE

I really want to come to school today...

...but I've picked up a really bad case of mistletoe poisoning. Believe me, you don't want me spreading this around the school. No one will have any of their toes left.

Book 10: Christmas Excuses

BONUS: BAD BREATH EXCUSE

I've got horrific morning breath . . .

. . . I need a chocolate pallet cleanser as a Christmas breakfast. But what should I choose? Chocolate coin, chocolate log, advent calendar chocolate or the biggest chocolate from the Christmas tree?

BONUS: NO TIME EXCUSE

Sorry, there's no time to do the Christmas washing up . . .

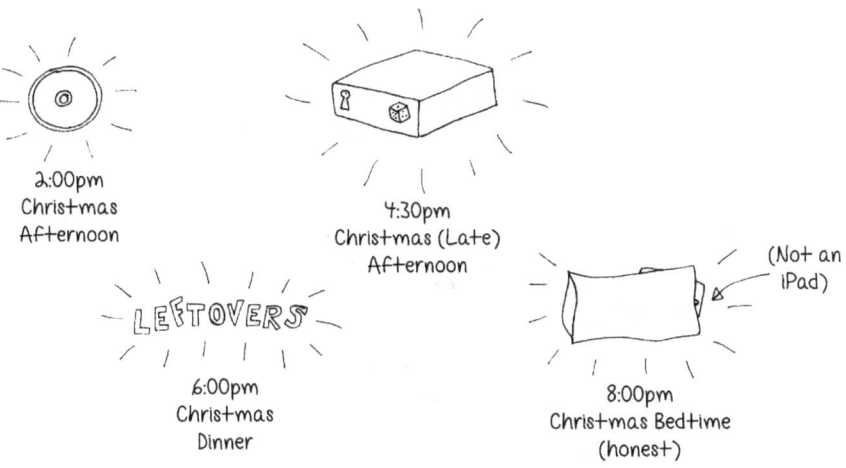

. . . I've got a very busy schedule. We'll just have to do the washing up next year.

Book 10: Christmas Excuses

BONUS: EXTENDED EDITION EXCUSE

Before we go to bed, let's watch one more Christmas film . . .

. . . How about the Home Alone Trilogy Extended Edition with an extra five hours worth of deleted scenes. Someone better go and make everyone some coffee as we're in for a looooooooong night.

BONUS: YELLOW PAGES EXCUSE

To catch Father Christmas I've made a number of Yellow Page Ads . . .

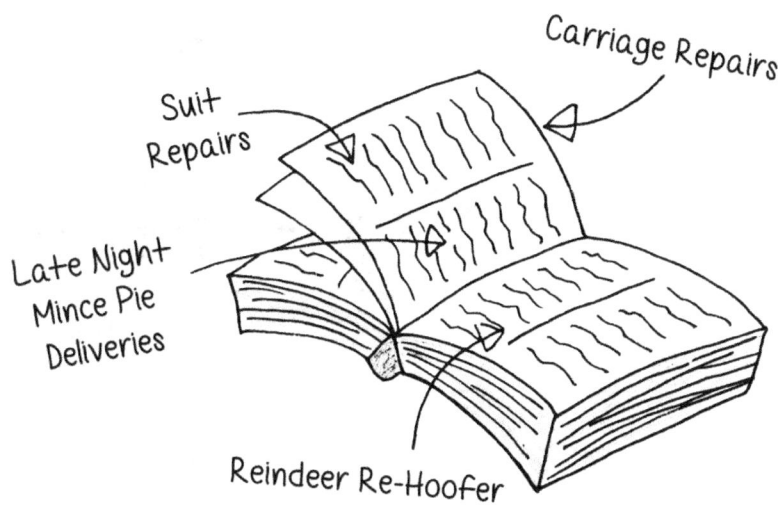

. . . I'm hoping to get a call from the jolly red-suited man. If he needs a pit stop later tonight, and I'll be ready.

Book 10: Christmas Excuses

BONUS: CHRISTMAS EXAM EXCUSE

Wake up, wake up . . .

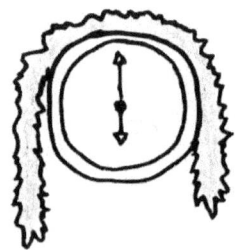

. . . the Christmas Exam is about to begin. It's a forty-five minute written exam followed by an all-day practical. You will receive your results on Boxing Day. If you pass I'll give you a hug every day for a whole year. If you fail I'll make it my mission to make sure you never touch the TV Remote for a whole year! Good luck.

The Excuse Encyclopedia

BONUS: CHRISTMAS STRESS EXCUSE

I am the GREATEST GIFT GIVER of all time .

. . . and in order for me to work my magic I need the four weeks before Christmas off school. And if you grant me this leave of absence. I'll make sure your gift is the best one.

Book 10: Christmas Excuses

BONUS: HANUKKAH EXCUSE

Christmas only lasts one day...

...However, I have just discovered that Hanukkah lasts for eight days. So, I'm now Jewish and need eight times as many presents than last year.

BOOK ELEVEN

Home-Schooling is the Future

Book II: Holiday Excuses

1. THE TREE-SCHOOL EXCUSE

Have you heard the news? A new school has opened at the bottom of the garden . . .

. . . Our old treehouse has been converted into a brand-new school especially for me. The curriculum is cartoons and the lunch break is 8 hours long. And the best bit is that no other children are allowed in and absolutely no teachers either.

2. THE SELF-TEACHER EXCUSE

I know what you are thinking. How can a child also be a teacher? . . .

. . . Let me answer that question with another question. Are there any teachers in the history of the Education System who have NOT consulted the *All-Knowing-Teacher*. I'm simply cutting out the middle-man. Go on. Ask me the hardest question you can think of and I'll reply with the correct answer.

Book II: Holiday Excuses

3. THE TV EDUCATION EXCUSE

Let me introduce you to my new teacher.

. . . I call her Teacher-Vision. In the morning she shows me the current affairs (the News Channel), then she teaches me important daytime knowledge (Daytime TV Shows), and then in the afternoon, she introduces me to economy and advanced maths (the Shopping Channels).

4. THE CLEVER EXCUSE

Now that I've learnt everything I can from big school my superior intellect is needed at home...

... So, grab a pen and paper, take a seat and start learning from my amazing mind.

Book II: Holiday Excuses

5. THE TEACHER OF HOMES EXCUSE

I've mastered the art of Home Schooling.

... These rebellious and ninny nincompoop numbskull homes all need a good teacher. So, I've decided to don the tweed and inspire them to grow up to become successful and happy homes. It's going to be my life's work.

New Business Ventures

Book II: Holiday Excuses

6. THE AWAY DAY EXCUSE

I've been doing some thinking. School kids get to go on all sorts of amazing trips . . .

. . . So I've set up a company called *Teacher Away Days*. So far I've got planned a trip to the Pencil Factory, the hill where some old bloke in history said 'charge' and then ate a sandwich, and the centre of an active volcano. The very first trip is on the first day of school. How would you like to go on a two-week expedition to the moon?

7. THE SUPPLY TEACHER EXCUSE

The animals at the zoo always look bored and the Supply Teachers at school always look overworked . . .

. . . So, I've created a business that encourages a job swap with local schools and local zoos. A hyena would make a great Geography Teacher because the subject is a joke. A parrot would make an excellent French Teacher because it can speak fluent gibberish. And a monkey would make a fantastic headteacher because if you're naughty in class you would get something even worse than a detention thrown at your face.

Book II: Holiday Excuses

8. THE ONLINE PUPILS EXCUSE

See you later, I'm going to school . . .

. . . Let me introduce you to my summer holiday invention – the Remote Controlled iStudent. While I stay at home in my warm bed this wonderful machine will go to school for me. Thanks to the web camera and microphone I can fully participate in every single lesson. Plus, if this thing works, I'm going to be a millionaire.

9. THE WORK EXPERIENCE EXCUSE

I'd love to come back to school, but first I have to complete my work experience...

...First, I'm at the Car Wash for six weeks, then the Supermarket for six weeks, then the Bank for six weeks, and then the Chocolate Factory for the rest of my life. So, if you stay in my good books, I'll wash your car, get you a discount on your groceries, re-mortgage your house and supply you with free chocolate for life. Do we have a deal?

Book II: Holiday Excuses

10. THE HAMSTER HEADTEACHER EXCUSE

While everyone was off school for the summer holidays the Headmaster was sacked and replaced by a hamster...

... The Hamster Headmaster is our new dictator. It makes the school rules now and it told everyone to go home and go back to bed. The teachers are right, budget cuts are the best!

Got a New Job

11. THE ADULT MINDER EXCUSE

I can't go back to school because kids aren't my target audience for my new public service...

... Do you have an adult who needs supervising? Then contact 'The Adult Minders' the new service that provides award-winning adult care run by fully qualified responsible children.

12. PROFESSIONAL ICE CREAM TASTER EXCUSE

I can no longer devote my time to education...

... I have an extremely important full-time job that requires my full attention. I taste and review ice cream for a living. I know what you're thinking, it's a tough job but someone has got to do it.

13. THE INJURY LAWYER EXCUSE

Did you have an accident while on your summer holiday that wasn't your fault? . . .

. . . Then call me and I'll help you get an extra month off school without any homework.

14. THE SCHOOL CARETAKER EXCUSE

Right, I'm off to work as the new School Caretaker...

... I've already changed the lock on the staff room door, persuaded the dinner ladies to spit in the headteachers coffee and swapped the toilet paper in the students' toilets for triple-ply with a hint of tea tree. Now then, off I go to open a second-hand jumble sale in the playground to sell off all the lost property so that I can buy a flat-screen TV for the caretaker's room.

Book II: Holiday Excuses

15. THE SECRET AGENT EXCUSE

Bye, I'm off to school now . . .

. . . *[whisper]* but I'm secretly working for the government as a secret agent to uncover a conspiracy that could cripple the National Education System, but I'm actually at the centre of that same conspiracy working against the government as a mole so that we bring down the National Education System from within.

Major Change in the Education System

Book II: Holiday Excuses

16. THE NEW WORLD ORDER EXCUSE

Haven't you heard the news? The whole world has been invaded and conquered by massive alien robot pigeons . . .

. . . Everyone has to stop going to school or work and instead go outside and play in the park, drop chips on the floor and comb our new overlords metallic feathers. It's what the alien robot pigeons want.

17. THE VICTORIAN REGRESSION EXCUSE

Haven't you heard the news? The government has reverted all our laws back to the Victorian Era . . .

. . . All children over the age of five have to go to work in factories, shine shoes or sweep chimneys. I choose the last one because I thought I'd get to tap dance across the rooftops of London like they do in Mary Poppins, but I was wrong.

Book II: Holiday Excuses

18. THE VIKING INVASION EXCUSE

Haven't you heard the news? The Vikings have invaded, again . . .

. . . At first, they only came back because they had left their phone chargers, but now that we've got good 5G coverage they've decided to stick around and rule over us with tyranny, cruelty and constant Facebook messages about the latest Ikea catalogue.

19. THE SCHOOL OF LIFE EXCUSE

Haven't you heard the news? All schools have been shut down by the government and children are to follow in their parent's footsteps instead . . .

. . . You caught me practising with your shoes. So, I've got to come to work with you and learn your trade. Let's go to work. (Note: this will only work if your parents are not School Teachers, Classroom Assistants or a Dinnerlady).

20. THE SCHOOL INSPECTORS EXCUSE

Haven't you heard the news? The School Inspectors closed the school due to poor standards...

... I have to wait in my pyjamas until another letter arrives from the Education Board to tell me which school I have to go to instead. Let's hope the postal service is as slow and unreliable as it always has been.

Unexpected Delay to Your Holiday Abroad

21. THE NEGOTIATOR EXCUSE

Here's the deal, Miss Print. I'll not come back to school . . .

. . . That's right. I'll make your life so much easier by not being in your classroom and all you need to do is tick my name on the register every day. But be warned, if you don't take my deal I'll ask 5 extremely awkward questions a day, here are a few to wet your appetite (for inspiration see *49 Questions to Annoy Your Parents*).

22. THE SCHOOL IN BERMUDA EXCUSE

Dear Teacher. With regret, I write to you from Bermuda to inform you I am not coming back to school . . .

. . . After going to the Caribbean for my summer holiday I decided to attend the local school, who have offered me a job. I am Professor of Sunbathing and Afternoon Naps. It was an offer I couldn't refuse. See you in a year!

Book II: Holiday Excuses

23. THE TIME-ZONE EXCUSE

What are you talking about. Summer hasn't just finished, it's just begun . . .

. . . I've decided to change time zones to Australia's, which means while you're all just finishing your summer holiday I'm about to start mine. I'm off to go and throw another shrimp on the BBQ. See you all in six weeks.

24. THE GLOBAL WARMING EXCUSE

Bad news everyone. Global Warming is here which means it's going to always be summertime...

... Which means autumn will never arrive. Which means it will always the summer holiday. Which means it will never be the start of school ever again. My advice, move to the beach and start stockpiling sun cream.

25. THE EXTENSION LETTER EXCUSE

Didn't you hear? I applied for a summer holiday extension . . .

BEST LETTER EVER!

. . . It was accepted, of course. What is the extension for? I didn't manage to sleep in past 1 pm, finish reading the Harry Potter series (both the books and the films) or master a new dance move. See you in two weeks.

Too Clever for School

26. THE UNI EXCUSE

Hi and bye . . .

. . . I know this is the first day back after the summer holidays but I just came to say goodbye. I'm so brainy I've been given a scholarship to Oxford University seven years earlier. I'll be Prime Minister in no time, at which point I'm going to make my first policy change to double the school summer holidays.

27. THE SPECIAL CLASSROOM EXCUSE

See ya, I'm off to McDonald's...

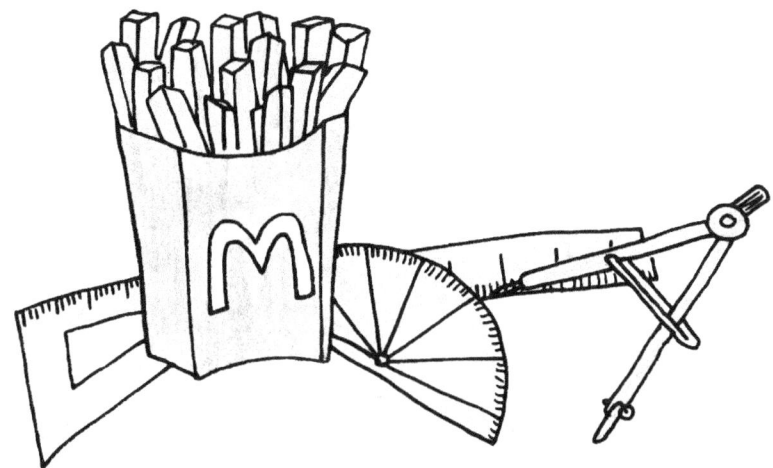

...Didn't you know? My old school tragically burnt down over the summer holidays. Thankfully the kind and generous fast-food chain offered their restaurant as our temporary classroom. Now I can have fries with my maths work.

Book II: Holiday Excuses

28. THE BITTEN EXCUSE

I was bitten by the ghost of Albert Einstein and now I'm super intelligent...

... In fact, I'm now so clever that I can now predict the future. You're going to agree with me that it's pointless I go back school and then we're both going to eat chocolate and watch TV.

29. THE NEW SYLLABUS EXCUSE

As I am the smartest kid in school I was asked to rewrite the school syllabus...

... And here it is – the new and improved Silly Bus. All aboard, next stop is another six week holiday at the beach.

Book II: Holiday Excuses

30. THE TEACHER SCHOOL EXCUSE

Welcome to your first day at Teacher School...

... The world has finally realised that age has nothing to do with intelligence and so have decided to make certain adults go back to school. As I'm so brainy I've been appointed as your new teacher. Finish class is Dodgeball. We're going to have so much fun.

Struck Down by an Illness

Book II: Holiday Excuses

31. THE MADE-UP EXCUSE

Don't look this up in the dictionary, but I have Tyrani-nanni-hyper-biscuit-itus . . .

. . . It's a terrible illness where I think I'm an angry old person who only eats biscuits. Please may I be excused so I can go back to the old peoples home and shout at the TV until I fall asleep?

32. THE ALLERGIC TO TEACHERS EXCUSE

The doctors have discovered why I hate school so much. It's because I'm allergic to teachers . . .

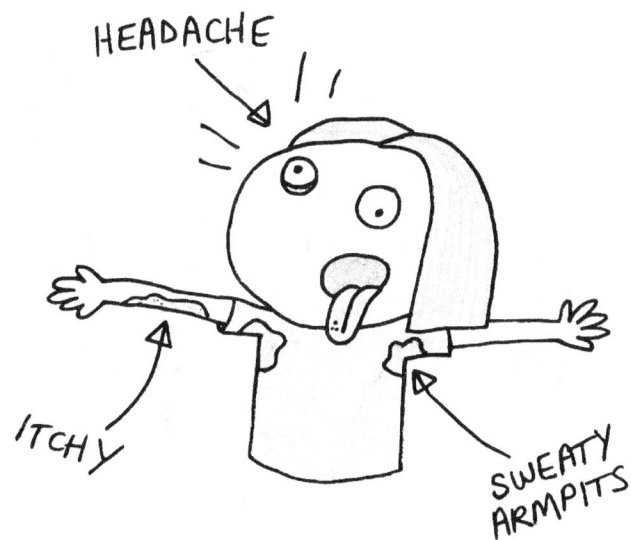

. . . When you think about it, it all makes sense. Whenever I'm in a classroom I get itchy. When the teacher asks me a question I get a headache. And when I hear the word *homework* I get hot and sweaty and my vision goes blurry and I start to blackout. Maybe I should go lay down at least a mile away from any teachers.

Book II: Holiday Excuses

33. THE ANTI-INSOMNIAC EXCUSE

You know how I'm always falling asleep in your classes . . .

. . . Well, turns out it's not because of your teaching style, it's because I'm an Anti-Insomniac. That means I'm tired ALL the time. I've been ordered by the doctor to spend all year in bed so I just came into school to say see you all next academic year. Night night.

The Excuse Encyclopedia

34. THE UNCOMMON-COLD EXCUSE

Don't come near me. I've caught an uncommon cold . . .

. . . It's exactly the same as a common cold except for one small difference. You get 100% more snot. There aren't enough tissues in the world to stop these two green rivers. Evacuate the classroom for your own safety. Anyone who can't swim, it was nice knowing you.

Book II: Holiday Excuses

35. THE D & V & E.L.F EXCUSE

I can't come back to school as I've been signed off by the doctor with D & V & E.L.F . . .

. . . Never heard of it? Its full name is diarrhoea and vomiting and extremely lethal flatulence. Uh oh. If everyone doesn't clear out of this classroom in the next 10 seconds you'll also get a demonstration.

Holiday Drama That Won't Let Up

36. THE SKIING ACCIDENT EXCUSE

Is it possible to break every bone in your body? . . .

. . . I almost managed it. I skied into a tree and broke 203 out of 206 bones. I'll have to do my school work from the hospital by blinking at a computer screen. Thank God I didn't break my eyelids!

The Excuse Encyclopedia

37. THE LOST MY PASSPORT EXCUSE

You know how people say never lose your passport while on holiday? . . .

. . . I've found out why. It's because if you do lose your passport in a foreign country you're stuck there until you find it again. So, I'll try to make it back before Christmas but I've got the whole of Disneyland to search for my passport, including all of the rides and attractions.

38. THE ADOPTED BY LIONS EXCUSE

Whilst on Safari in Africa I learnt that Lions are very loving parents...

...After they ate my mum, dad and older sister they were full and so adopted me as one of their own. That's right, I'm a lion cub now. I think it would be best to let me skip the first few months of school and I'll persuade my new parents not to maul you to death at the next parents evening.

The Excuse Encyclopedia

39. THE FELL DOWN A WELL EXCUSE

My name is Timmy and I fell down a well.
. .

... Unfortunately, the Fire Brigade is on holiday, Lassie is having a manicure and my parents are enjoying the peace and quiet.

Book II: Holiday Excuses

40. THE STILL QUEUING EXCUSE

I've finally reached the middle of the queue to go on Space Mountain! ...

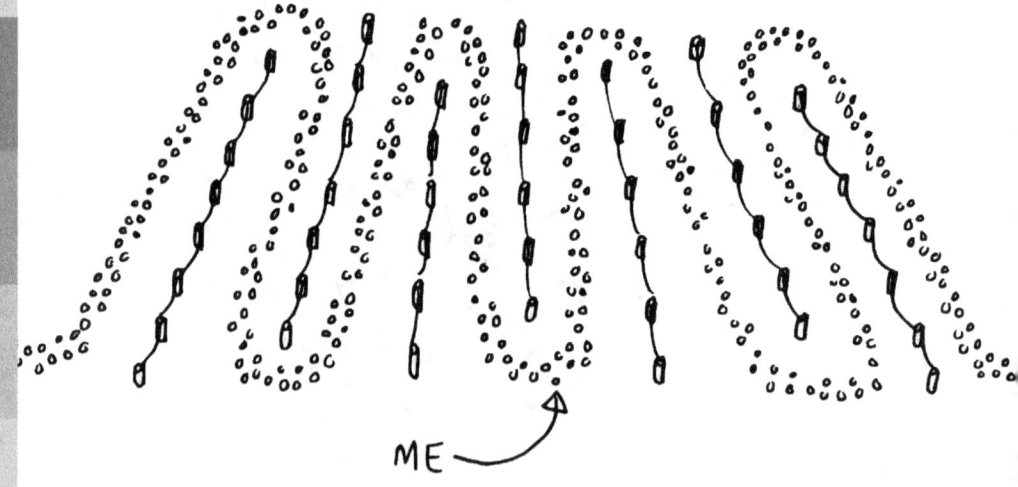

ME

... I can't go to school now. It would be a terrible waste of all this time if I leave the queue. I'll let you know if the rollercoaster was worth the three-week queue in one to two weeks time.

Rich Kids Don't Need No Education

Book II: Holiday Excuses

41. THE BOARDING SCHOOL EXCUSE

Now that my parents are filthy rich they're sending me to Boarding School...

... I am going to learn how to wear a sandwich board, how to write on whiteboards and how to shout 'All Aboard' like a Train Driver. No more English or Maths or stinky Geography for me.

42. THE SET FOR LIFE EXCUSE

The best thing about being filthy rich is that I'll never have to work a day in my life...

... So that means school is a waste of time for a rich kid like me. I think I'll go learn how to drive a speed boat instead of going to my French Lesson.

Book II: Holiday Excuses

43. THE BOUGHT THE SCHOOL EXCUSE

Great news, Miss. My filthy rich parents bought the school over the summer holidays...

... They want all the teachers to reapply for their jobs and have appointed me to do the job interviews. Your gruelling interview will be in two weeks so you better go and get practising.

The Excuse Encyclopedia

44. THE SUBSTITUTE PUPIL EXCUSE

Teachers are always getting Substitute Teachers when they can't teach...

...So I've been able to hire and pay for a Substitute Pupil. His name is Boris and he is the smartest kid in the world. He actually knows what all the buttons on a scientific calculator are for. I'm going to go for a nap while Boris takes this test for me.

Book II: Holiday Excuses

45. THE MISSION TO MARS EXCUSE

I'm not coming back to school because I have become a Martian...

...I'm leaving Earth to become the first kid to live on Mars. Please, please tell me there's no school on Mars.

Extremely Silly Excuses (that probably won't work)

46. THE SPECIAL BUTT EXCUSE

I've been saying it for years and now its official, my butt is special . . .

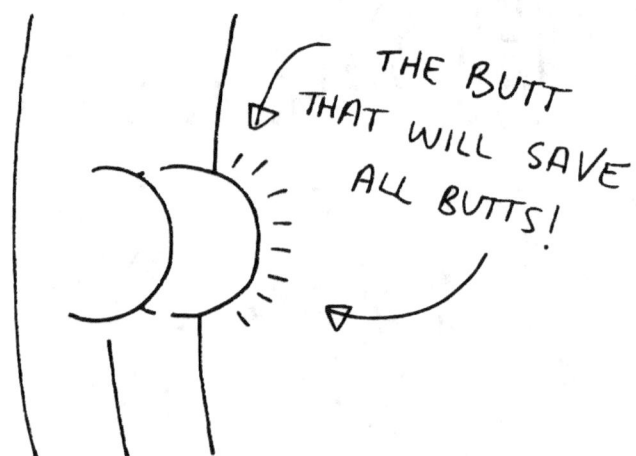

. . . Scientists from around the globe have all been applauding my behind and it's incredible powers. Apparently, my farts could be the key to beating world hunger, reversing climate change and curing cancer. If you need me I'll be in a secure top-secret laboratory trumping to save the planet.

47. THE PSYCHIC EXCUSE

I really would love to come back to school but what's the point when the world is going to end in five days . . .

. . . My psychic told me that there is an asteroid, an alien invasion and a deadly plague all heading for the earth that will destroy all humankind. On the bright side that gives me enough time to finish watching all my TV shows. Enjoy your last days of existence.

Book II: Holiday Excuses

48. THE DATE DYSLEXIA EXCUSE

School started two weeks ago? Really!?..

... The doctor said this would happen. I've been told I have Date Dyslexia which means I can never work out which day of the year we are on. To be honest I thought it was either Christmas, Halloween or Dress Like a Unicorn Day. I feel like a complete idiot now.

The Excuse Encyclopedia

49. THE COUNTDOWN EXCUSE

I'm here, I'm on time and I'm ready to learn...

CHRISTMAS BREAK

SPRING BREAK

SUMMER HOLIDAY

...I understand that school is important for my future but, don't forget, holiday breaks are just as important for my mental health. So I've created this helpful countdown. 75 Schools Days to the Xmas Break. 139 School Days to the Spring Break. 199 Schools Day to next years Summer Holiday. Bring on the learning!

Book II: Holiday Excuses

BONUS: LIBRARY CARD EXCUSE

I'm so excited for the first day back at school...

LIBRARY CARD

...Don't forget, you need to drop me off at the library now instead of school. That's where I'll be meeting my new one-to-one tutor (called YouTube).

BONUS: NEW SUPPLY TEACHER EXCUSE

Over the summer holidays I had an epiphany . . .

. . . The animals at the Zoo always look extremely bored and and the Supply Teachers at school always look extremely overworked. So, I've started a initiative that encourages job swaps between local schools and the nearby Zoo.

Book II: Holiday Excuses

BONUS: GALACTIC APPRENTICESHIP EXCUSE

Good news, I don't have to go back to school...

...I got accepted onto an Apprenticeship Course. Apparently, my midi-chlorian count is very high which means I can go into a star ship and travel across the galaxy to the Jedi Temple on Coruscant.

BONUS: NO MORE EXAMS EXCUSE

The school exams have been updated...

...All of the exams are now 100% practical and require 0% revision time. So, that means no more studying all night and no more stupid lined paper or red-hot hand cramp from hours and hours of writing.

Book II: Holiday Excuses

BONUS: PRIZE WINNINGS EXCUSE

Look Miss, I've been very busy over the summer holiday . . .

. . . I won the Nobel Prize, the Booker Prize and 1,352,759 Arcade Coupons. With all this prize money I'm set for life.

BONUS: INDEPENDENCE EXCUSE

I developed a condition over the summer holidays which means I can no longer attend school . . .

. . . It's called 'Independence'. I've realised I don't need to attend school to be a happy and successful human being. Now then, I'm going to go out into the world and make my fortune. Which way to Vegas?

Book II: Holiday Excuses

BONUS: WARDROBE EXCUSE

Lucy, Edmond, Susan and Peter all thoroughly enjoyed their summer holiday in a wardrobe . . .

. . . But when I tried it I had an awful time. I am still lost. Please send a search party. And the worst part is I haven't found any Turkish Delight.

BONUS: CASH IN THE BAG EXCUSE

Teachers often complain about two things . . .

. . . 1. Having too much money, and 2. Having to deal with annoying kids, like me, who just keep on coming back. Well then, give me $1,000 and I can solve both of those problems.

BONUS: RUNNER FOR LIFE EXCUSE

Over the summer holiday I started running, and I've decided to never stop...

... You know, like Forrest Gump. So, until someone works out how to attach four wheels and an engine to my school I can't continue my education.

The Excuse Encyclopedia

BONUS: PLASTIC NINJA EXCUSE

I can't come back to school because I've joined the fight against plastic pollution...

...I'm waging war on the non-biogradable, non-recyclable, ocean-destroying plastic polluting our world (and you should all join me).

Book II: Holiday Excuses

BONUS: PILE OF UNATTENDED CASH EXCUSE

Oh look, a big pile of unattended cash . . .

. . . Now, if I was to go and take another six weeks holiday that would mean that you, my wonderful teacher, would be able to spend it on golden pencils, tea bags, potted plants and whatever else teachers like to spend money on.

BOOK TWELVE

Creepy Costume Ideas

HALLOWEEN EXCUSES

1. THE REAL-LIFE VAMPIRE EXCUSE

I don't want to scare you, but these are my normal eyes and I'm not wearing fake teeth . . .

. . . Yep, that's right. I'm a real-life vampire. This is the one time of year I can walk around the neighbourhood without people screaming and sharpening planks of wood whilst calling their priest. So, give me some extra sweets and next time I'm *feeling thirsty* I'll steer clear of your house.

The Excuse Encyclopedia

2. THE FULL MOON EXCUSE

Quick, quick, quick. Give me candy and QUICK! . . .

. . . It's a full moon tonight and the only way to stop me from turning into a werewolf is letting me eat as many sweets as I can. Quickly, I can already feel the wolf hairs sprouting out of every inch of my body and my fingernails growing sharper by the second.

Book 12: Halloween Excuses

3. THE WITCHES CAULDRON EXCUSE

Do you like my witch costume? . . .

. . . I've tried to be as authentic as possible, with an actual wand and full-size cauldron too. You'll need to give me LOTS of candy to fill this thing. Also, do you have any spare wheels?

4. THE SKELETONS EXCUSE

My name is Barry, and this is Harry and Sally . . .

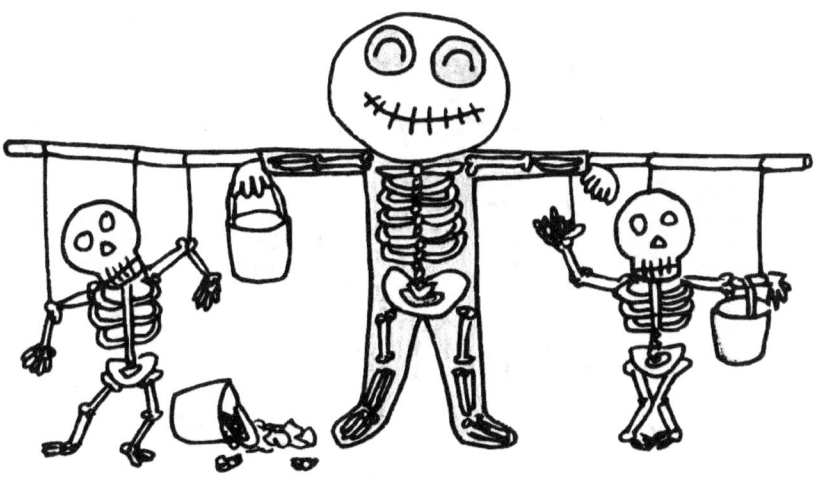

. . . We are all living, breathing children who need lots of candy. By the way, Barry likes liquorice but the rest of us think it tastes like grandmas three-day old socks.

Book 12: Halloween Excuses

5. THE GRIM REAPER EXCUSE

Hi, I'm the Grim Reaper . . .

. . . You know, the dude who turns up when someone is about to die, points his bony finger and, WHAM, they're dead. However, I do have a very sweet tooth and I could be persuaded to pass you by if a huge pile of candy were to suddenly appear in front of me.

Handy, but Spooky Inventions

HALLOWEEN EXCUSES

Book 12: Halloween Excuses

6. THE HOOVER EXCUSE

Oh, thank goodness. You've still got plenty of sweets left . . .

. . . Now then, it's time to show you my wonderful *Halloween Invention*. If you would be so kind as to open the lid of the sweets and I'll switch on my super spooky suction machine.

7. THE TRAINED HAMSTER EXCUSE

I've been working on my Halloween costume all year . . .

. . . I'm dressed as Doctor Frankenstein and this is my pet zombie hamster. Oh no, my hamster has lost control. He has jumped into your house and is chewing all your expensive furniture. I'll look after your candy bowl while you go catch my zombie hamster.

Book 12: Halloween Excuses

8. THE EGG LAUNCHER 3000 EXCUSE

Isn't she magnificent! I call her the Egg Launcher 3000...

... This beautiful little contraption can launch 120 eggs in a minute at speeds of over 60mph and distances of over 100 metres. Alas, I may not be able to even use it. Isn't it a shame that if everyone is generous giving out candy tonight then I will not get to switch it on?

9. THE GHOSTBUSTER EXCUSE

I don't want to alarm you but there is a *ghost* in your house . . .

. . . Fear not, for I am a trained and licensed Ghostbuster. I'll catch the ghost in exchange for all your remaining candy.

10. THE CANDY DETECTOR EXCUSE

You've run out of candy? Are you sure you don't want to change your answer? . . .

. . . My Candy Detector is telling me there is a cake in your fridge, Haribo in the attic and chocolate bars stashed under the floorboards. I can wait here while you get me something, preferably the chocolate, please.

The Perfect Technique

HALLOWEEN EXCUSES

Book 12: Halloween Excuses

11. THE STICKY EXCUSE

I am ready to pick out my candy . . .

. . . Before I do so a quick word of warning. I'm going to struggle to adhere to the one candy rule. You see, I have naturally sticky fingers.

The Excuse Encyclopedia

12. THE ART OF DISTRACTION EXCUSE

Trick or WOOOOOW WHAT IS THAT BEHIND YOU!!!?!!! . . .

. . . *[While their back is turned grab what you can]* Sorry, I thought I saw a ghost. Well then, best be off now that my candy bag is full. Bye.

Book 12: Halloween Excuses

13. THE SLEIGHT OF HAND EXCUSE

I understand. You have a strict one candy per child rule...

... Has anyone ever told you that you have a lovely hallway? [While they giggle with joy from the fake compliment, take a handful of sweets and hide it up your sleeve]. That's a delightful lampshade. Well then, I'll take my one allotted candy and bid you farewell.

14. THE MOONLIGHT SERENADE EXCUSE

Hello. I'm a zombie who enjoys playing the harp . . .

. . . You look stressed. Sit down, relax and enjoy the soothing sounds of my harp serenading you in the moonlight as you peacefully doze off for a nap. Don't worry, I'll look after the candy while you are asleep.

Book 12: Halloween Excuses

15. THE HALLOWEEN YOGA EXCUSE

Hello and welcome to Halloween Yoga . . .

. . . Just because it's the spookiest night of the year doesn't mean you have to feel stressed. Join me, your Mummy Yoga Instructor, in the Corpse Position. Lie down and still your body and mind. Breathe in as you ignore the hand rummaging around for candy. Breathe out as I run away with as many sweets as I can carry.

Turning Halloween into a Business

HALLOWEEN EXCUSES

Book 12: Halloween Excuses

16. THE FRANCHISING EXCUSE

This year I had an epiphany...

... Instead of running around collecting candy on my own I should teach other kids my amazing techniques and, in return, receive 10% of their profits. I now have enough sugar to give my whole school diabetes.

17. THE TRADE EXCUSE

I hear adults enjoy eating fruit and vegetables and children enjoy eating sweets and chocolate...

... Let's make a trade. My bowl of fruit and veg for your bowl of Halloween candy. And I'll throw in this Magikarp Pokemon Card free of charge, which happens to be one of the rarest Pokemon trading cards in the world.

18. THE TRUST-WORTHY KID EXCUSE

Tonight I'm offering a fantastic service .

. . . Every time you open the door a horrible draft blows up your dressing gown. Give me your candy and I'll evenly distribute them between all the kids in the neighbourhood so you can watch that TV series you've been looking forward to with a nice cup of tea in peace.

19. THE PRICELESS OFFER EXCUSE

Listen carefully, I'm about to offer you something priceless . . .

. . . I, your friendly neighbourhood kid, will give you all the gossip on the street, unlimited access to the play park supervised by me and my gang, and I'll grass up my friend who stole your garden gnome. All you need to do is give me the rest of your candy. This is a once in a lifetime offer, so what will it be?

Book 12: Halloween Excuses

20. THE C.E.O. EXCUSE

Good evening, it's time for your Audit . . .

C.E.O. of HALLOWEEN

. . . As C.E.O. of Halloween, I have been checking your neighbourhood to ensure the high sweets standards I expect are being met. So please hand over all your remaining candy for inspection.

Forgot to Dress in a Costume?

HALLOWEEN EXCUSES

21. THE MUGGLE EXCUSE

But I am dressed for Halloween. I'm a *muggle*...

... You know, non-magic folk. There are too many kids dressing up as wizards and witches these days so I thought I'd make sure the muggles get fair representation this year.

22. THE TRAGIC ACCIDENT EXCUSE

I lost my parents in a tragic Halloween-related accident . . .

. . . I don't want to talk about it. I'd rather drown my sorrows in sweets and chocolate.

Book 12: Halloween Excuses

23. THE MATHS TEACHER EXCUSE

For Halloween this year I decided I would dress in the scariest costume I could think of...

...I'm dressed as a Maths Teacher! I am knocking on people's doors to collect super impossible algebra homework. Scary costume, right!

24. THE VR GOGGLES EXCUSE

What are you talking about, I have made an effort. I'm wearing a *VR Halloween Costume* . . .

. . . What's VR, you ask. It stands for *Virtual Reality* and means you've got to wear these special goggles to see my amazing and realistic computer-generated Frankenstein costume. Now put down that big bag of candy and put on these goggles.

Book 12: Halloween Excuses

25. THE NIGHTMARE EXCUSE

I know I'm not wearing a costume. Its because I don't want to scare you . . .

. . . Not yet. You see, I'm a living nightmare. So, if you don't give me lots of candy I'll crawl into your head while you're sleeping and haunt your dreams for the rest of your life.

White Lies (with a tiny smudge of black)

HALLOWEEN EXCUSES

Book 12: Halloween Excuses

26. THE SICK OLDER SISTER EXCUSE

Please sir, give generously to my sick older sister...

...This might be her last Halloween before she becomes extremely hormonal, starts growing armpit hair and sprouts disgusting spots all over her face. Help make her *last* Halloween special by giving her all your candy!

27. THE BEST COSTUME EXCUSE

Do you like my costume? . . .

. . . Thanks. You do know that you are supposed to give extra candy to the kid with the best costume, right? It's the most ancient and sacred rule of Halloween.

28. THE SUGAR-FREE KIDS EXCUSE

I'm sorry to interrupt but I have some very important information...

...The kids who are behind me are severely diabetic. That means if a gram of sugar touches their tongue they could lose all their fingers and toes and Minecraft experience points. I'll help by taking all your sugary candy and you can take these cardboard flavoured cardboard snacks to give them when they knock on your front door.

29. THE RULE BREAKER EXCUSE

Oh dear oh dear oh dear. Breaking the rules I see . . .

. . . That's a non-regulation door handle, a serious lack of spooky decorations and no sign on your door. I could be persuaded not to tell the Halloween Official Ruling Body if, say, you were to give me all your remaining candy.

Book 12: Halloween Excuses

30. THE BROOMSTICK EXCUSE

What? I'm a kid from this neighbourhood . . .

. . . I'm Jenny, the Henderson's daughter who lives at number 125. I've been using my motorised broomstick to travel up and down the street because I've broken my leg and not to travel around the whole town collecting candy across all the neighbourhoods. That would be cheating.

Extremely Silly Suggestions

HALLOWEEN EXCUSES

Book 12: Halloween Excuses

31. THE QUINTUPLETS EXCUSE

What? No, I have not come knocking on your door five times in five different costumes . . .

. . . I'm an identical quintuplet. Fred is dressed as a mummy, Carl as a vampire, James as a dementor, Logan as an undead lollipop lady and I'm a ghoul with bad dress-sense. Can I have my candy now?

32. THE SPIDERS EXCUSE

Hello, do you know the story of the Pied Piper? . . .

. . . Well, I'm dressed as the Halloween Pipe Piper. When I start playing my spooky tune on this pipe I can either rid your home of spiders or, I can fill your home with spiders. Your choice, which will heavily depend on the quantity of candy you give me.

Book 12: Halloween Excuses

33. THE YOUR PARENTS EXCUSE

Hi *son/daughter*. That's right, I'm dressed as your strict, overbearing parents . . .

. . . Now go get ready for sleep at once, it's well past your bedtime.

The Excuse Encyclopedia

34. THE VENDING MACHINE EXCUSE

Do you like my costume? I'm the human Vending Machine from hell . . .

. . . I don't accept candy. Instead, you have to insert money and then I'll give the candy to myself.

Book 12: Halloween Excuses

35. THE UNLUCKY LEPRECHAUN EXCUSE

I just can't take it anymore. What's an Undead Leprechaun without a pot of gold? . . .

SOB SOB SOB

. . . Hang on, do I see chocolate coins? Well, thank my lucky stars. You're a Halloween Angel. Thank you.

Less Candy, More Money

HALLOWEEN EXCUSES

Book 12: Halloween Excuses

36. THE DIABETIC EXCUSE

Oh no. You've only got sugary candy...

... I'm a diabetic werewolf which is a condition that causes high levels of glucose in my blood because of a lack of insulin. Don't feel bad, I'll accept cash, cheque or PayPal payments instead.

37. SPONSORED CANDY FEAST EXCUSE

Hi, will you sponsor me in my Halloween Challenge . . .

. . . I'm raising money for kids who can't afford sweets by doing a sponsored *eat as much candy as you can in one evening* challenge. You can either donate money or sweets, your choice.

Book 12: Halloween Excuses

38. THE COINS EXCUSE

Only coins, please . . .

. . . No, no. Not chocolate coins. Actual real coins that I can use to buy actual tasty sweets from an actual sweet shop.

39. THE 10P A DAY EXCUSE

Thanks for the free candy but I have a different idea...

...Just give me 10p per day for the rest of your natural life. (If twenty neighbours agree and give you a 10p every day for 10 years you'll be £7,300 richer).

Book 12: Halloween Excuses

40. THE CANDY SHOP OWNER EXCUSE

Right then, what you got on offer? . . .

. . . I've just become a Candy Shop Owner and I'm planning to open my shop in the playground on Monday. I need marshmallows, strawberry laces and foam bananas. Don't worry, I can wait here while you pop to the shops, if needed.

Too Cute to Say No

HALLOWEEN EXCUSES

Book 12: Halloween Excuses

41. THE UNDEAD CHOIR EXCUSE

We've decided to spread some Halloween cheer by going from door to door singing carols . . .

. . . Which Halloween Carol would you like us to sing? *Another Noël in the Coffin, Love at First Bite* or *Ghouls Just Want to Have Fun?*

42. THE READING EXCUSE

Tonight I have been treating the neighbourhood to a dramatic reading...

...I have the three most terrifying books in my hand. *Macbeth, Frankenstein's Monster or the Minecraft Bible.* You may choose which one I read in exchange for loads and loads of candy.

Book 12: Halloween Excuses

43. THE FAMILY PET EXCUSE

Have you met our family pet? . . .

. . . Meet Slimy the pet slug. He was dressed as a zombie ninja but he ate his costume. It was my fault for making it out of lettuce. Anyway, if you want you can look after him while I continue trick or treating.

44. THE DRAWING EXCUSE

I made you a Halloween drawing . . .

. . . This is you ruling over the whole neighbourhood as everyone knows you're the nicest and most generous neighbour in the world. In fact, tonight would be a wonderful opportunity to prove it by giving out the most candy, don't you think?

Book 12: Halloween Excuses

45. THE GLOW IN THE DARK EXCUSE

For my costume to work it has to be pitch black outside . . .

. . . You see, I'm a glow in the dark pumpkin. Nobody's going to give me handfuls of candy until they see me in all my glowing splendour.

Stay Out Later, Get More Candy

HALLOWEEN EXCUSES

Book 12: Halloween Excuses

46. THE NOCTURNAL EXCUSE

I plan on collecting a record-breaking amount of candy this year...

...How? By knocking on doors throughout the night until dawn. It fits with my costume, you see, Vampires are nocturnal. I can crawl back into my coffin once the sun comes up.

The Excuse Encyclopedia

47. THE MASTER PLAN EXCUSE

Ok, here's the plan . . .

. . . Hit the village at *Happy Hour*, go all the way down Main Street in the *Witching Hour*, come back down the other side in the *Slug Hour* and finish in Section B in the *Tipsy Hour*. Stick to the plan and I'll have the biggest bag of candy in the whole neighbourhood by 10 pm.

Book 12: Halloween Excuses

48. THE OPTIMUM TIME EXCUSE

I have done intensive research and discovered something amazing . . .

. . . The exact time when your neighbours will be the most generous when giving out candy on Halloween is 8:32 pm. Quick, jump in the car and drive me to the Duke of Westminster's house (the richest man in the world) and we should just make it in time.

The Excuse Encyclopedia

49. THE THANK YOU EXCUSE

Hello, I'm the Spider Princess. Trick or treat...

... *[once you've received the candy, choose one of the following which is most appropriate to each house and neighbour]*

1. Thank you very much *[then pause and smile sweetly]*.
2. Thank you, I love all of your Halloween decorations, very spooky.
3. Thank you for your generosity and kindness, and happy Halloween. *[It may not work at every door, but those two magic words showing you are a polite young citizen will undoubtedly earn you extra treats]*.

Book 12: Halloween Excuses

BONUS: DEMENTOR'S KISS EXCUSE

Have you ever watched or read Harry Potter?...

... Then you'll know that a Dementor's Kiss will suck out your soul. So then, pucker up or hand over the candy.

The Excuse Encyclopedia

BONUS: HIDING PLACE EXCUSE

Everywhere I've knocked so far has run out of candy! . . .

. . . I put extra effort into making this amazing costume this year *[with lots of concealed storage pockets to hide candy]*. I'm so sad. If only there was some way you could cheer me up. Perhaps something chocolatey with sprinkles on top.

Book 12: Halloween Excuses

BONUS: CUTE (DEMON) CHILD EXCUSE

Trick or treat. It's the cutest child you've ever seen . . .

. . . (but, if you don't give me lots and lots of candy, I'll put on my other costume and turn into a DEMON CHILD whose head spins around and around with a scream that will burst your ear drums and molten vomit that will melt your face off).

BONUS: WICKED WITCH EXCUSE

This year I'm going to scare the candy straight from your hands . . .

. . . I've been intercepting your mail all year. You had a lot of junk mail, a few letters, and these beauties. They're your bills!!! I think the red one looks particularly scary.

About the Author

About the Author

James Warwood is a writer and illustrator who lives on the borders of North Wales with his wife, two sons, and cactus (called Steve the Cactus).

He has a degree in Theology, which at the time seemed like a great idea, until he released he didn't want to become an RE Teacher. Instead, he writes laugh-out-loud middle grade fiction and non-fiction. He also fills them with his silly cartoons. He is the bestselling author of the EXCUSE ENCYCLOPEDIA and the TRUTH OR POOP SERIES.

James likes whiskey, squirrels, reading silly books, playing his bass guitar, and Greggs Sausage Rolls. He does not like losing at board games or having to writing about himself in the third person.

The Excuse Encyclopedia

Discover Other Middle-Grade Fiction Books by James Warwood:

The Chef Who Cooked Up a Catastrophe

The Boy Who Stole One Million Socks

The Girl Who Vanquished a Dragon

Where to find James online:

🌐 www.cjwarwood.com
ⓕ James Warwood
🐦 @cjwarwood

www.ingramcontent.com/pod-product-compliance
Lightning Source LLC
Chambersburg PA
CBHW072042110526
44590CB00018B/3004